Financial Accounting:
A MERCIFULLY BRIEF
Introduction

Michael Sack Elmaleh

Financial Accounting:
A Mercifully Brief Introduction

By Michael Sack Elmaleh, CPA, CVA, MS, MA

Illustrated by Jeremy David Delaval Willis

Published by Epiphany Communications
12529 Molasses Rd, Union Bridge, MD 21791

ISBN: 0-9764744-0-9

Printed in the United States of America

Library of Congress Cataloging-in-Publication Data
Elmaleh, Michael Sack

Financial accounting: A mercifully brief introduction/Michael Sack
Elmaleh
p. cm
Includes index
ISBN: 0-9764744-0-9

Visit our home page at http://www.epiphanycommunications.com

About the Author

Nearly thirty years of practical accounting experience have erased most of the ill effects of the author's formal education. That education included a BA in psychology and philosophy, an MS in accounting and an MA in philosophy all from the University of Wisconsin. As revenge on academia, the author has served as an adjunct instructor at three colleges, teaching courses in accounting, economics, finance, statistics, and mathematics. Currently, the author is trying to figure out how to get over the ill effects of nearly thirty years in accounting. Writing this book has helped.

Acknowledgements

The author would like to thank Jed Sanborn, CPA, Robert Walter, and Joseph Sack for reviewing early drafts of this text and offering valuable suggestions and encouragement. I also thank students in my accounting classes who alerted me to the need for this book. Special thanks go to my most talented copy editor, Barbara Wyatt, who despite an incredibly demanding schedule, made time to insure that no comma was misplaced or omitted. Thanks also to my illustrator, Jeremy Willis; who had an uncanny knack of capturing precisely the bizarre visual images I needed to supplement this text. The quotation of Frank Knight is taken from Peter Bernstein's *Against the Gods: The Remarkable Story of Risk*, John Wiley and Sons, Inc.

Foreword: Why a Mercifully Brief Introduction to Accounting?

Most introductory accounting texts focus very heavily on the mechanics of accounting. Much attention is given to journalizing transactions, getting the debits and credits in the right place, and compiling financial statements in the proper form. Today, even the smallest business can afford reasonably good accounting software that handles the bookkeeping mechanics adequately. What accounting software cannot do is interpret the information contained in financial statements.

The emphasis on mechanics leaves relatively little time, particularly in compressed learning formats to question the quality and usefulness of financial statement information. These are the issues, I think, small business owners and non-accountants most need to explore.

In order to address the meaning of financial statement information, some understanding of bookkeeping mechanics is required, but not to the extent included in traditional textbooks. This book explains just enough of the mechanics needed to consider the reliability and usefulness of accounting information.

This book also differs from the traditional texts in another way. When traditional introductory texts discuss the uses of financial statements, the focus is almost exclusively on the **positive** value of the information content. Not nearly enough attention is given to the **limitations** of accounting information. In this era when stock prices react wildly to every slight fluctuation in reported or expected quarterly earnings, it is important for non-accountants to begin to appreciate these limitations. This book discusses financial accounting's strengths *and* weaknesses.

Finally, many, if not most, introductory accounting texts use examples from large and small businesses. In this book I have chosen to introduce the fundamental principles of financial accounting in the context of small businesses only. I have done this for two reasons. First, I believe that the small business environment is easier for non-accountants to understand. Second, small firms comprise about 99% of the over 40 million businesses that are now operating in the United States. Marketing considerations suggest a book to benefit this larger market.

Contents

**Measurement problems are sometimes
more than accountants can bear.**

In This Chapter

- Just What is Economic Performance
  and Economic Condition?

- Money: Accounting's Unstable
  Measurement Unit

- Measurement Error: Management's
  Motivation for Mendacity

- Why Bother With Accounting at All?

- The World According to GAAP

Accounting's Surprisingly Difficult Measurement Problems

" Oh, well, if you cannot measure, measure anyhow."
Frank Knight

Financial accounting consists of the rules and procedures used to measure the economic performance and condition of a business firm. The most widely used rules are **Generally Accepted Accounting Principles** (GAAP). GAAP strives to answer two basic questions: how did the business do last year, and what did the business own and owe at the end of the year? The answers to these questions are summarized in two basic reports, the **income statement** and the **balance sheet**. The income statement lists revenue earned and expenses incurred during the year. The balance sheet lists asset, liability and equity amounts as of the end of the year.

If you have even a passing knowledge of business and economics answering these questions might not seem that difficult. In fact, determining a firm's economic performance and condition often is very difficult. Unfortunately, financial statements rarely are able to give completely definitive and precise answers to what seem to be simple economic questions. Why would this be so?

Accounting's measurement problems derive primarily from three factors that I will discuss briefly. First, it is difficult to pin down exact criteria for measuring economic performance and economic condition. Second, accounting uses money as its fundamental measurement unit, and money's unit value is not stable over time. Third, accounting rule makers have to allow for the fact that business managers often are motivated to distort economic reality rather than reflect it accurately.

Just What is Economic Performance and Economic Condition?

In terms of economic performance, our simplest criterion for doing well surely involves looking at cash flows. A business does well if it brings in more cash than it spends and vice versa. But as you will soon see, for all but the very simplest of businesses such a measurement approach can be very problematic.

As shown in a later example, negative cash flow is not necessarily equivalent to poor economic performance and vice versa. Because of these problems accountants have had to develop a more abstract concept of economic profitability which creates its own problems.

Accounting encounters even more difficulty in trying to pin down a firm's economic condition. To determine economic condition we want to find out about the firm's assets and their values. But there is more than one standard of value. Should accountants use current market values for assets owned or the original cost incurred to acquire them? Rarely are these values the same and there are advantages and disadvantages to both standards.

There also is legitimate controversy about what should be counted as assets on the balance sheet. For example, should the value of personnel or intangible assets, such as patents, trademarks and goodwill, be measured and included? If so, how do we measure their value?

Money: Accounting's Unstable Measurement Unit

In accounting the unit of measurement is money. Money is a medium of exchange that has value only to the extent that it can be traded for goods and services. But, money is not a stable unit of measurement because its exchange value varies with time. What one dollar buys today in goods and services is almost never the same as what that same dollar purchased last year or will purchase two years from now. Such changes in the exchange values of money are referred to as inflation or deflation depending upon the direction of the change.

The practical ramifications of this instability of money as a measuring unit are pervasive. If a company had net income last year of $100,000 was its economic performance the same as it was five years ago when its income statement also showed a $100,000 net income? Decidedly not, if the purchasing power of the dollar changed significantly in the intervening five years.

Questions about economic condition are also affected by the instability of money as a measurement unit. For example, consider two companies each with $800,000 of assets and $500,000 of liabilities. In the case of one company all its debt must be repaid within one year, while the other company's debt does not have to repaid for ten years.

Are the economic conditions of the companies the same? Again, decidedly not, because the purchasing power of the dollar will change over the next ten years.

GAAP rule makers have struggled greatly with the questions of how and when these changes in the value of money should be reflected.

Measurement Error: Management's Motivation for Mendacity

Measurement error is unavoidable. But it would be nice if we could assume that almost everybody involved in the accounting measurement process was highly motivated to avoid errors. Sadly this is not the case because business managers often wish to avoid accurate measurements if such accuracy would lead to significant damage to their career and finances. Facing such ruin managers will be strongly tempted to avoid fair and accurate measurements. Managers will seek to "cook the books".

There are two important ramifications for accounting stemming from this motivational bias. First, in order for financial reports to have any credibility at all they have to be verified by independent auditors. This is an expensive and often imperfect process. Second, in formulating GAAP, the rule makers have to carefully consider how any proposed measurement procedures might be subverted by managers intent on providing a skewed view of economic performance or condition. The practical consequence of this is that the accounting rules that might be most logical and simple are often not adopted because these rules also tend to be the easiest ones for managers to manipulate.

If Reliable Accounting Measurements Are So Hard To Achieve, Why Bother With Accounting at All?

Accounting measurements, despite the inherent limits discussed throughout this book, usually can assist in reliably evaluating the economic performance and condition of a business. But in order to achieve a more comprehensive evaluation of a business *economic information not included in financial statements must be considered.*

You cannot accurately assess the economic condition or the performance of a business by simply looking at its financial statements.

You must combine financial statement information with information about the economic environment in which the business operates. You must understand the firm's products and services. You must know about the firm's competitive position. You must understand the risks the business faces. And you sometimes have to make assessments about a firm's strengths and weaknesses that cannot easily be quantified.

The World According to GAAP

Generally Accepted Accounting Principles (GAAP) were not handed down to the accounting profession from God through some Old Testament prophet. Rather, the accounting profession has delegated to a series of committees the responsibility for promulgating specific rules. Currently the responsibility falls to the Financial Accounting Standards Board (FASB).

The Securities and Exchange Commission (SEC) is a regulatory agency of the federal government that can also set accounting principles for companies whose shares trade on various stock exchanges. Historically, the SEC has not intervened in setting accounting rules but has left the task largely to the FASB. Occasionally even the Congress has attempted to intervene in setting accounting rules.

Who Enforces GAAP?

Any company that is listed on a stock exchange has to prepare its financial statements in conformity with GAAP. Independent Certified Public Accountants (CPAs) must be hired to audit these accounting records and financial statements to insure that these statements have been prepared in conformity with GAAP. GAAP acquires its leverage through these auditing requirements. Failure to provide financial statements in accordance with GAAP would jeopardize the credibility of a firm's financial statements and adversely affect the price of company stock.

Generally, non-publicly traded private businesses have no legal obligation to follow GAAP in preparing financial accounting reports. Non-publicly traded companies sometimes are required to use GAAP by banks or other lenders who require access to periodic financial reports. Sometimes these lenders require that CPAs audit these financial statements. Small firms often use GAAP rules for generating financial statements on a voluntary basis because these rules provide the best framework for developing useful information about economic performance and condition.

Chapter 2

Accounting is not for the weak kneed.

In This Chapter

- The Fundamental Accounting Equation
- Accounts: Sub-Categorical Imperatives
- Revenue and Expenses and Equity: Articulating the Connection

The Balancing Act:
Assets = Liabilities + Equity

Businesses usually own assets. **Assets** are things that can be used to generate revenue through the sale of goods and services. Assets include cash, inventory, furniture and equipment, and accounts receivable. A business may also own intangible assets such as patents, trademarks and goodwill.

GAAP assumes that all assets of a business are either owned outright by the business owners or are subject to the claims of creditors. Creditors are anyone that has loaned money to the business. Loans and other forms of extended credit are called **liabilities**. The portion of assets not subject to claims by creditors is called **equity**.

In the GAAP framework there must be a continuous equilibrium between assets on the one side and the total of liabilities and equity on the other side. This is represented by the fundamental equation of accounting:

Assets = Liabilities + Equity

This equation is also the basis for the most basic of accounting reports, the aptly named **Balance Sheet**. A balance sheet reports what a business owns (assets), what it owes (liabilities) and what remains for the owners (equity) as of a certain date. This equation must always be in balance.

Examples:

If a business has $1,000 of assets at a particular time those assets must be matched by the total of the claims of creditors and owners. Here are two of an infinite number of acceptable balance sheets:

The El Maroq Co. Balance Sheet	
Assets	$ 1,000
Liabilities	$ 500
Equity	500
Total Liabilities and Equity	$ 1,000

The Raqco Co. Balance Sheet	
Assets	$ 1,000
Liabilities	$ 800
Equity	200
Total Liabilities and Equity	$ 1,000

It is possible for liabilities to exceed assets. If so the equity must be negative for the total of liabilities and equities to equal the positive total assets.

The Lowe Co. Balance Sheet	
Assets	$ 1,000
Liabilities	$ 1,100
Equity	(100)
Total Liabilities and Equity	$ 1,000

A business whose liabilities exceed its assets is termed **insolvent**.

Equity as Residual Claims

In the GAAP framework equity is simply the difference between assets and liabilities. The owner has positive equity only to the extent that assets exceed liabilities. If a business has $1,000 of assets and $600 of liabilities the $600 of liabilities are, in effect, a claim on the assets. Equity is the difference between the assets and liabilities, or $400.

Equity = Assets - Liabilities

By common law, if a business ceases operations the priority claims on assets go to outside creditors. The claims of owners can be realized only after outside creditors' claims are satisfied. As such, equity represents the owners' residual claim on business assets.

Accounts: Sub-Categorical Imperatives

The fundamental accounting equation analyzes a business in terms of three categories: *assets, liabilities* and *equity*. It is useful to break these categories into sub-categories called *accounts*. Here are typical accounts by category. Detailed descriptions and examples of accounts will be found in later chapters of the book.

Assets

Cash: The balance of coins and currency on hand and funds held in checking, savings and money market accounts.

Accounts Receivable: Customers' promises to pay later for goods or services already provided.

Prepaid Expenses: Payments toward an expense that a business will not benefit from until some time later, e.g., a one-month rental deposit.

Inventory: Goods sold to customers.

Fixed Assets: Tangible assets expected to last over a year that enable a business to provide goods or services.

Liabilities

Accounts Payable: A firm's promise to pay later for services or goods already received.

Notes Payable: Loans made to a business.

Withheld Taxes: Taxes withheld from employees' wages.

Accrued Payroll Taxes: Employer's share of payroll taxes owed.

Deferred Revenue: Cash collected by a business now for services or goods to be provided later, e.g., a year's magazine subscription collected by a magazine publisher in advance.

Equity

The equity section of a balance sheet has different account names, depending upon the legal structure of the business. A business may have *unlimited liability* or *limited liability*. Limited liability businesses include corporations, limited liability companies (LLCs), or limited liability partnerships (LLPs). The distinguishing feature of a limited liability firm is that the owners' personal liability for firm actions is limited to the amount they have invested. Usually such businesses have to be registered or incorporated in a particular state and must comply with that state's laws regarding its legal structure.

Unlimited liability firms include sole proprietorships and general partnerships. In these firms the owners have unlimited liability for the actions of the business. The distinction between limited and unlimited liability businesses boils down to the extent to which an owner can be sued for the actions of the business.

Example. The *Threadbare Tire Company* has manufactured tires that were so defective that certain customers lost life and limb in various car accidents. Suppose the estates of the deceased successfully sued the company for $5 million. Let's further suppose that Threadbare has net business assets of only $3 million.   If Threadbare were a limited liability company, the owners would have no obligation to pay the $2 million needed to satisfy the remaining judgement against the company. If, on the other hand, *Threadbare* were an unlimited liability company, the owners would be responsible for satisfying the remaining judgement.

Proprietorship Equity

An unincorporated business with one owner is a **sole proprietorship**. Its equity categories are broken down as follows:

Owner's Equity: Cash or property contributed to a business by its owner.
Owner's Withdrawals: Cash or property distributed to an owner from the business.

Partnership Equity

An unincorporated business with more than one owner is a **partnership**. If a partnership has two owners, the equity section would contain the following accounts:

Partner A Equity: Property or cash contributed by partner A to the partnership.
Partner A Withdrawals: Property or cash distributed by the partnership to partner A.
Partner B Equity: Property or cash contributed by partner B to the partnership.
Partner B Withdrawals: Property or cash distributed by the partnership to partner B.

Separate pairs of similar accounts would be required for any additional partners in the partnership. Sometimes Owner or Partnership Equity accounts are labeled "Partner Capital" or "Owner Capital". Owner or Partnership Withdrawals accounts are sometimes labeled as simply "Owner Draws" or "Partner Draws".

Shareholder Equity

A limited liability business is usually called a *corporation*. Its owners are called *shareholders*, because they are issued *common stock* certificates that represent their share of ownership in the business. The equity section of an incorporated business would be broken down into at least these sub-accounts:

Common Stock: The original amount of cash and/or property shareholders contribute to a business in exchange for common shares.
Dividends Paid: Cash or property paid to shareholders from business net income.
Retained Earnings: The amount of net income not distributed to shareholders.

Revenue and Expenses and Equity: Articulating the Connection

There is a close relationship between the economic condition of a business and its economic performance. Generally, businesses that do well, end up well off. Good performance generates a good economic condition. Profits generate assets; losses eat up assets and generate liabilities. This connection between economic performance and economic condition is built into the basic accounting equation, which always requires that assets equal the sum of liabilities and equity.

Changes in Equity: Revenues and Expenses

Changes in equity occur when the owner contributes to or draws money from the business. But such transactions are relatively infrequent. More frequently changes in equity occur through earning *revenue* and incurring *expenses*.

A business generates revenue when it exchanges goods or services with its customers in return for money or other assets. A business incurs expenses by exchanging its assets for goods and services it needs to generate revenue. A business realizes net income or profit if its revenues exceed expenses. If its expenses exceed revenue, the business incurs a loss.

Revenue and expenses are sub-categories of equity. In generating revenue and expense, assets and liabilities are always effected. For example, if a business renders a service in exchange for cash, assets (cash) increase. However, to maintain the basic accounting equation, either the liability or the equity side must increase by an equal amount. But in selling services no liability is incurred. So this means that equity must increase. *An increase in revenue must lead to an increase in equity.*

Similarly if a business incurs a cash expense, an asset, cash, has decreased. So the other side of the accounting equation must decrease as well. Because paying cash to meet an expense is not equivalent to paying off a debt, there is no decrease in liabilities. So the incurring of an expense must be accompanied by a change in equity. In fact, *all incurred expenses lead to reductions in equity.*

Note that sometimes a business receives assets from lenders or from its owners. The receipt of such assets is *not* revenue. Only assets received from customers or clients in exchange for goods or services con- stitute revenue. Similarly, the disbursement of assets to repay loans or distributions to owners are not expenses. Only disbursement of assets used to generate revenue are considered expenses.

The table on page 15 illustrates the relationship between the basic categories in the accounting equation.

Revenue and Expense Accounts

Just as there are sub-categories of assets, liabilities and equity, there are numerous sub-categories of revenue and expense. The collection of all asset, liability, equity, revenue and expense accounts is called the *general ledger* accounts. Some of the more typical revenue and expense accounts are the following:

Revenue

Sales: income from selling goods to customers.

Interest Income: income from lending money or extending credit to customers.

Rental Income: income from leasing property.

Service Fees: income from the provision of services such as law, medicine, and accounting.

Expenses

Cost of Goods Sold: costs of products sold to customers.

Salaries and Wages: payments to employees for services provided.

Rent: payments for the use of real property.

Utilities: payments for heating, electric, and other utility services.

Office Expense: a broad category of expenses related to office administration.

Payroll Taxes: the employer's share of Social Security, Medicare and unemployment taxes associated with salaries and wages.

Professional Fees: costs of services provided by outside advisors, such as attorneys and accountants.

Advertising: costs associated with the promotion of a firm's products or services.

Phone: costs for telephone services.

Repairs and Maintenance: costs of repairs and maintenance to property and equipment.

Travel: costs for use of automobiles, other transportation, and lodging expenses associated with business travel.

Meals and Entertainment: costs of business related meals and entertainment.

Depreciation: the portion of a fixed asset's original cost recognized in a specific accounting period.

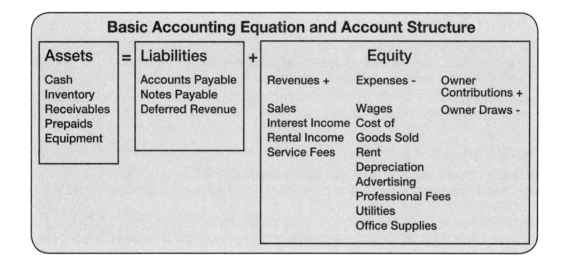

The Income Statement

Even though revenue and expense transactions change equity, the specific changes in revenue and expense account balances are reflected in a separate fundamental financial statement called the *income statement*.

Sometimes the income statement is referred to as the *profit and loss statement* or simply the "P & L". The income statement addresses the question of economic performance. Did the firm do well (make a profit) or do badly (incur a loss)? The earning of revenue and incurring of expenses is so central to the operation of a business that it requires this separate report to monitor operating results.

The income statement reflects the changes in the revenue and expense accounts over a certain period, usually not more than a year, or less than a month. The balance sheet, on the other hand, reports the assets, liabilities and equity at a specific point in time, usually at the end of a year, quarter or month.

Example. Mort Thanatopolis, a licensed mortician, has decided to open a funeral home specializing in very low cost funerals. The business will be called "*Can U Dig It?*" Here is a list of his first month's cash transactions:

December 1, Mort opens a business checking account with a deposit of $5,000 of his own funds.
December 3, Mort pays $1,000 for 1,000 extra large, heavy duty, plastic bags.
December 5, Mort borrows $1,500 from his sister Morticia.
December 5, Mort purchases $500 of newspaper advertising.
December 8, Mort collects $1,200 in fees for three funeral services.
December 9, Mort pays $155 to a local minister to officiate at the three funerals.
December 10, Mort uses 3 plastic bags at the funerals.

The table below illustrates the effect of these transactions on the fundamental accounting equation:

| | Assets | | Liabilities | Owners Equity | |
Transaction	Cash	Funeral Supplies	Note Payable	Mort Capital	Type of Equity Transaction
1-Dec	5,000			5,000	owner investment
3-Dec	(1,000)	1,000			
5-Dec	1,500		1,500		
5-Dec	(500)			(500)	advertising expense
8-Dec	1,200			1,200	service revenue
9-Dec	(155)	-	-	(155)	contract labor
10-Dec	-	(3)	-	(3)	funeral supplies
Balances	6,045	997	1,500	5,542	

Notice that the basic accounting equation is maintained after each transaction. In the first transaction an asset is increased by $5,000 while equity increases by the same amount. In some transactions, like the second, only one side of the equation is changed. One asset, cash, decreased, while another asset, funeral supplies, increased by the same amount. In the third transaction, cash increased and so did a liability in the same amount. The final four transactions involved revenue and expenses, which are increases and decreases in equity.

The revenue transaction increased both cash and equity by the same amount. The expenses decreased both assets and equity by the same amount. These transactions and final account balances lead to the following simple balance sheet and income statement.

Can U Dig It?
Balance Sheet
12/31/04

Assets	
Cash	$ 6,045
Funeral Supplies	997
Total Assets	$ 7,042
Liabilities	
Note Payable	$ 1,500
Equity	
Mort Capital	5,542
Total Liabilities & Equity	$ 7,042

Can U Dig It?
Income Statement
For the Month Ended 12/31/2004

Revenue	$ 1,200
Expenses	
Funeral Supplies	3
Advertising	500
Contract Labor	155
Total Expenses	658
Net Income	$ 542

Summary

- Business firms have assets, liabilities and equity. Assets are the productive resources a firm uses to generate revenue. Liabilities are the firm's debts owed creditors. Equity represents the owners share of assets net of liabilities.
- At all times the fundamental equation must hold: Assets = Liabilities + Equity.
- Firms generate revenue from the sale of goods and services. In generating revenue the firm acquires assets like cash and accounts receivable. In order to generate revenue most firms must incur expenses which usually means the reduction in cash or increase in liabilities.
- Revenue increases owner's equity; expenses decrease owner's equity.
- The total of assets, liabilities and equity as of the end of accounting period is reported on the balance sheet. The revenue earned, and expenses incurred, during the accounting period is reported on the income statement.
- It is useful to breakdown assets, liabilities, equity, revenue and expense into sub-categories called accounts.

Exercises

1. Define assets, liabilities and equity.
2. Give two examples of accounts for each of the above.
3. What is the mathematical relationship between assets, liabilities and equity?
4. Define revenue and expense.
5. Give three examples of accounts from each of the above.
6. What is the relationship between equity and revenue and expense?
7. If a business has $5,000 of assets and $1,000 of liabilities what must its equity equal?
8. Is it possible for a business to have more liabilities than assets?
9. What are the advantages of limited liability businesses? Discuss briefly the societal costs and benefits to allowing limited liability businesses. Most states do not allow limited liability protection for professional services such as law, medicine and accounting? Why would these states deny these professionals such protection?

Problems

1. For the following transactions indicate whether owner's equity increases, decreases or stays the same:
   a. An owner contributes $500 to a business.
   b. A business purchases an asset for $1,000 cash.
   c. A business borrows $2,500 from a bank.
   d. A business collects $200 in revenue.
   e. A business incurs $100 of expense.

2. Rusty Blade opened a low budget surgery clinic called *Cut It Out*. After the first year of operations the business had the following asset, liability, equity and revenue and expense balances.

Cash	$27,400
Surgical Equipment	30,000
Note Payable	30,400
Blade Equity	5,000
Surgical Revenue	75,000
Salary Expense	35,000
Office Rent	12,000
Utility Expenses	2,400
Malpractice Insurance	3,600

Prepare the balance sheet and income statement for the business. Note that the ending equity balance must equal the owner's capital contribution plus the annual net income.

Chapter 3

Shoebox record keeping gives accountants *fits.*

In This Chapter

- Books of Original Entry

- Posting from Journals to General Ledger Accounts

- Debits and Credits

- Journalizing Transactions

Recording Transactions:
Taking Care of Business Every Day

Accounting ends with score keeping but begins with record keeping. The first task of accounting is to accurately record **transactions**. Transactions are events that change the composition of a firm's assets, liabilities, and equity.

Books of Original Entry

Record keeping is greatly facilitated if the details of transactions are recorded in writing. To insure accuracy the recording should take place when the transaction occurs. There are many ways transactions can be initially recorded: on little scraps of paper, on the backs of envelopes or, better yet, on specially designed registers or journals.

Transactions involving cash disbursements can be recorded on simple check registers, on check stubs or by use of checks that automatically create a copy of the original. The most accurate and reliable method of record keeping utilizes computer software to create and print checks. Such software automatically stores a complete record of the transaction as checks are generated. Cash receipts can be recorded on cash register tapes, or in deposit books that automatically create copies of the original deposit tickets.

The information captured from a recorded transaction is more important than the form used in recording it. At a minimum, the written record should include the date of the transaction, the parties involved, the dollar amounts disbursed or collected, and the nature of the transaction.

A **cash disbursements journal** is designed to capture all the important elements of each cash disbursement. Below is an example of a cash disbursements journal. The first column indicates the date of the payment. The second column indicates the check number issued. The third column indicates the party who received the payment (usually called the **payee**). The fourth column indicates the amount of the disbursement. Columns five through twelve represent account categories. Placing the amount of the payment in a specific account category column indicates the nature of the transaction. For example, the first check in the journal, written to La La Land Realty, is clearly for office rent because the amount of the payment is placed in that column.

Notice that the disbursement journal uses a **double entry format**. This means that the amount of the check is always placed in the fourth column and an equal amount entered into one of the account columns. The total at the bottom of column four must equal the total of columns five through twelve. This double entry is a control against mis-recording disbursement amounts.

Joint Ventures Cash Disbursement Journal

(1) Date	(2) Check #	(3) Payee	(4) Cash Amount	(5) Rent	(6) Advertising	(7) Prof. Fees	(8) Contract Labor	(9) Office Supplies	(10) Owner Draw	(11) Other	(12) Amount
1/3/2005	1001	La La Land Inc.	500.00	500.00							
1/5/2005	1002	High Times	275.00		275.00						
1/6/2005	1003	Shtuples	93.00					93.00			
1/8/2005	1004	Mesa News	45.00		45.00						
1/9/2005	1005	C. Marin	350.00				350.00				
1/10/2005	1006	Art Anderson	175.00			175.00					
1/11/2005	1007	Dull Computer	1,555.65							Equipment	1,555.65
1/12/2005	1008	J. Morrisin	1,200.00						1,200.00		
1/13/2005	1009	Shtuples	25.16					25.16			
1/14/2005	1010	C. Marin	350.00				350.00				
1/15/2005	1011	Mesa PD	1,500.00							Protection	1,500.00
1/16/2005	1012	Scoff Law SC	2,500.00			2,500.00					
1/17/2005	1013	J. Morrisin	1,200.00						1,200.00		
		Totals	9,768.81	500.00	320.00	2,675.00	700.00	118.16	2,400.00		3,055.65
		Control Total	9,768.81								

Cash disbursements journals, check registers, and cash receipts journals are referred to as **books of original entry**.

Posting from Journals to General Ledger Accounts

Information contained in these books of original entry must be transferred or **posted** to general ledger accounts. Recall that the collection of all accounts is called the general ledger. All general ledger accounts should be thought of as specially formatted records shaped as a big "T". For example think of the cash account as looking like this:

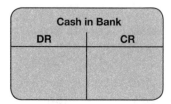

The importance of the "T" structure is that it distinguishes between the left and right side of each general ledger account. Here is the first rule of transaction posting:

Every transaction posting must involve a dollar entry on the left side of one account and an equal dollar entry on the right side of another account.

Because assets must always equal the total of liabilities and equity, any increase in one account must be offset with an equal change to another account that maintains this equation. Notice this does not mean that one account necessarily increases when another account decreases. For example if an asset account is increased, the accounting equation can be maintained by increasing a liability or equity account or by decreasing another asset account.

You can visualize this basic rule by looking at the teeter-totter illustration at the beginning of Chapter 2. For equilibrium to be maintained, the addition or subtraction of weight on one side of the teeter-totter must lead to some compensating addition or subtraction of weight. But the compensating addition or subtraction does not necessarily have to occur on opposite sides of the fulcrum. Let's say our toga-clad friend, who represents assets, acquires a gallon of wine. One obvious way to maintain the equilibrium of the teeter-totter would be to add some weight to the other side. However, we could also maintain teeter-totter equilibrium if Mr. Asset relieves himself immediately of just enough of his pre-existing weight to compensate for the addition of a gallon of wine, so his net weight after the acquisition of the wine remains unchanged.

When a dollar amount is posted to a specific general ledger account, the account's cumulative balance increases or decreases depending upon whether the posting is on the left or right side of the "T". However, postings on the left are not automatically considered increases, just as postings on the right are not automatically decreases. *Whether a posting on the left constitutes an increase or decrease depends upon the nature of the account.* Here are the rules:

Increases in asset and expense accounts are recorded on the left side of the "T", while decreases are recorded on the right side.

Increases in liability, equity and revenue accounts are reflected on the right side of the "T", while decreases are reflected on the left side.

The logic of these rules follows directly from the location of the accounts in the basic accounting equation. The left side of the accounting equation includes all the asset accounts and the right side contains all the liability and equity accounts. To increase an asset account, remember that the assets are on the left side of the fundamental equation, and so you record an entry on the left side of the "T". To increase an equity or liability account, remember that these accounts are located on the right side of the fundamental equation, and so you record an entry on the right side of the "T".

To decrease accounts in any category record them on the opposite side of the "T" from their location in the fundamental equation. For example, to decrease an asset account, which is on the left side of the equation, record an entry on the right side of the "T". To decrease a liability or equity account, record an entry on the left.

This reasoning also works for revenue and expense accounts. Recall that revenues are increases in equity and expenses are decreases in equity. Because equity is on the right side of the equation, record an increase in a revenue account on the right side of the "T" account. On the other hand, because expenses are decreases in equity, they are recorded on the left side of the "T".

Debits and Credits: Shorthand for Left and Right Sides of T Accounts

Accountants have developed a shorthand notation for the terms "left side" and "right side" in account balances. Instead of saying "left side" and "right side" they use the terms "debit" and "credit". "Debit" simply means the left side of the "T" account, and "credit" refers to the right side of the "T" account. But remember:

"Debit" does not always refer to an increase in an account balance nor does "credit" always refer to a decrease, or vice versa. Most importantly, " credit" does not refer to something good and "debit" to something bad. "Debit" means left, "credit" means right. In accounting that is all these terms mean.

Using these new shorthand terms we can now restate the basic posting rules:

A debit is an increase in an asset or an expense account and a decrease in a liability, equity, or revenue account.

A credit is an increase in a revenue, liability, or equity account and a decrease in an asset or expense account.

Most transactions posted to revenue accounts are credits. Most transactions posted to expense accounts are debits. Asset, liability, and equity account transactions have substantially equal amounts of increases and decreases. Thus they have a significant amount of both debit and credit postings. The typical cumulative end of period balances are as follows:

Normal Ending Account Balances

Asset Accounts:	**Debit**
Liability Accounts:	**Credit**
Revenue Accounts:	**Credit**
Expense Accounts:	**Debit**

If you want to become agile at analyzing and recording transactions you simply have to memorize these posting rules. Here is a table summarizing the posting rules:

Summarized Debit and Credit Rules		
Account Type	**To Increase**	**To Decrease**
Asset	Debit	Credit
Liability	Credit	Debit
Equity	Credit	Debit
Revenue	Credit	Debit
Expense	Debit	Credit

Remember that every transaction must involve a change in one account and an equal and offsetting change in another account so that the basic accounting equation is kept balanced. We can now restate the rule this way:

Every transaction involves at least one debit and one equal and offsetting credit. If there are more than one debits or credits in a transaction the total of the debits and credits must be equal.

Journalizing Transactions

All transactions are first recorded in books of original entry on specialized journals, such as the cash disbursements journal illustrated above. Another widely used journal is called the **general journal**. In most businesses this journal is used to record non-cash transactions. *For learning purposes only*, we will use the general journal to illustrate the recording of both cash and non-cash transactions.

A general journal format looks like this:

Date	Acct.#	Account Description	Debit	Credit

The date column refers to the date the transaction took place, not necessarily the date the transaction is recorded. The second column refers to the account number associated with the account. In traditional bookkeeping systems accounts are coded according to whether they are assets, liabilities, equity, revenue, or expense. One common scheme is to assign assets numbers between 100-199, liabilities, 200-299, equity 300-399, revenue 400-499, and expenses 500-599. The third column refers to the full name of the account. The next two columns indicate whether the account is to be debited or credited and in what amount. By convention the account to be debited is listed before the account to be credited. The term "credit" is often abbreviated "Cr", while "debit" is abbreviated "Dr" (from the German word "drek").

Examples of Basic Cash Transactions

Now that we know the basic theory and measurement conventions specified by GAAP we can analyze and record some common cash transactions.

Transaction 1. Jim Morrisin, a licensed pilot, starts an air transport company called *Joint Ventures*. The company specializes in delivering agricultural products between Central America and the southern United States via small planes. His business will be organized as a proprietorship. He invests $10,000 of his own money and opens a checking account.

This transaction consists of an increase in cash and an offsetting increase in owner's equity and should be recorded like this:

Date	Acct.#	Account Description	Debit	Credit
1/5/2004	101	Cash in Bank	$10,000	
	301	Owners Equity		$10,000

Notice the slight indentation of the Owner's Equity account. This slight indenting of the account that receives the credit emphasizes the credit is the right side of the entry while the debit is the left side of the entry.

Notice also that the transaction maintained the basic accounting equation in that the left side (assets) increased by $10,000 and the right side (liabilities and equity) increased by the same amount.

Transaction 2. Jim leases a small plane for $1,000 a month. The entry for the first month's rent looks like this:

Date	Acct.#	Account Description	Debit	Credit
1/5/2004	510	Equipment Lease	$1,000	
	101	Cash in Bank		$1,000

This transaction involves an expense and an asset. Again, the fundamental equation is maintained. A decrease in an asset (cash) is offset by a decrease in equity. Remember that expense accounts are sub-categories of equity, and that the increase in the Equipment Lease expense decreases equity.

Transaction 3. Jim receives his first delivery order from a Mexican farmer to ship several kilos of product from Mexico to San Antonio. He receives $5,000 for making the delivery. The entry is:

Date	Acct.#	Account Description	Debit	Credit
1/25/2004	101	Cash in Bank	$5,000	
	401	Revenue		$5,000

The increase in an asset (cash) has been offset by an equal increase in equity (revenue).

Transaction 4: Jim withdraws $3,000 from the business for personal living expenses. The entry is:

Date	Acct.#	Account Description	Debit	Credit
1/31/2004	302	Owner's Draw	$3,000	
	101	Cash in Bank		$3,000

The decrease in assets (cash) is offset by a decrease in equity (owner's draws reduce equity). Note that in an unincorporated business distributions to owners are not treated as expenses. Such draws constitute reductions in equity.

All journal entries, whether made in the general journal or in a specialized journal such as the cash disbursements journal, must be posted to the appropriate general ledger account.

Here is what the general ledger "T" accounts look like after posting the above journal entries:

Cash in Bank			Owners Equity	
DR	**CR**		**DR**	**CR**
10,000	1,000			10,000
5,000	3,000			
15,000	4,000			

Equipment Lease			Transport Revenue			Owners Draw	
DR	**CR**		**DR**	**CR**		**DR**	**CR**
1,000				5,000		5,000	

Notice that the ending balance in the cash account is a debit of $11,000, because the total debits of $15,000 exceed the total credits of $4,000.

Analyzing Transactions

Here is some guidance on analyzing and recording common transactions.

The most common transactions involve revenue and expense accounts. When a firm sells products or provides services it earns revenue, so a revenue account must be increased. This means a revenue account must receive a credit. The offsetting debit is always to an asset account; most commonly Cash or Accounts Receivable. When a firm incurs an expense, an expense account must receive a debit. The offsetting credit is almost always either to Cash or to Accounts Payable.

The next most common transactions involve cash payments and receipts associated with Accounts Payable and Accounts Receivable.   An accounts payable is a liability the firm incurs in exchange for goods and services it receives. When the firm makes a cash payment to reduce such a liability, Accounts Payable receives a debit and Cash receives the off-setting credit. An accounts receivable is a customer's or client's promise to pay for goods or services it has previously received. An accounts receivable is an asset. When the firm receives a payment from the customer to repay their account, Accounts Receivable receives a credit and Cash receives the offsetting debit.

Less frequently the firm will be involved in *financing transactions*. In a financing transaction the firm is either receiving or repaying a loan. When the business receives the loan the Cash account is debited and the Notes Payable account is credited. When the firm makes a repayment the Notes Payable account is debited and Cash is credited. This is the correct posting for repayment of loan principal. Interest payments on loans are expenses and the correct entry for the repayment of interest is a debit to the Interest Expense account and an offsetting credit to Cash.

The acquisition of fixed assets is another class of relatively infrequent trans-actions. When a firm acquires a fixed asset such as equipment or office furniture the appropriate asset account is debited. The offsetting credit is to Cash if the firm pays for the asset immediately or Notes Payable if the payment will be deferred until after the acquisition.

Finally, there are the infrequent transactions between the firm and its owners. Usually these involve cash transfers to and from the owners. If an owner is contributing cash to a firm Cash is debited and an appropriate equity account such as Owner's Equity is credited. When a firm distributes cash to owners Cash is credited and an account such as Owner's Draws is debited.

The above types of transactions do not exhaust the possible types of transactions but account for the most common activities that a business engages in.

Another Example of Cash Transactions

Just for practice, let's look at some more transactions and postings.

On 1/3/05 Hamlet, an MSW, decides to open a psychotherapy clinic. He contributes $5,000 to the business. The $5,000 is an increase in cash to the business, so cash must be increased (debited). Since the cash comes from the owner, the credit must be recorded in an equity account.

Date	Acct.#	Account Description	Debit	Credit
1/3/2005	101	Cash in Bank	$5,000	
	301	Owners Equity		$5,000

On 1/03/05 Hamlet borrows $15,000 from his friend Rosenkrantz to furnish his office and defray other start up costs. The business receives $15,000 cash and now owes $15,000.

Date	Acct.#	Account Description	Debit	Credit
1/3/2005	101	Cash in Bank	$15,000	
	210	Notes Payable		$15,000

On 1/4/05 Hamlet pays $1,500 rent for his office. Cash is decreased and an expense, rent, increases.

Date	Acct.#	Account Description	Debit	Credit
1/4/2005	510	Rent Expense	$1,500	
	101	Cash in Bank		$1,500

On 1/4/05 Hamlet purchases office furniture for $9,100. Office furniture is an asset, so this asset increases, while another asset, cash, decreases.

Date	Acct.#	Account Description	Debit	Credit
1/4/2005	110	Office Furniture	$9,100	
	101	Cash in Bank		$9,100

On 1/29/05 Hamlet collects $8,000 in patient fees from his HMO. An asset, cash, increases. He has earned these fees, so the offsetting entry is an increase to revenue.

Date	Acct.#	Account Description	Debit	Credit
1/29/2005	101	Cash in Bank	$8,000	
	401	Service Fees		$8,000

On 1/30/05 he draws $3,500 for living expenses. Since Hamlet is drawing the money to defray **personal** expenses the disbursement is considered an owner's withdrawal, which is a decrease in owner's equity.

Date	Acct.#	Account Description	Debit	Credit
1/30/2005	310	Owners Draw	$3,500	
	101	Cash in Bank		$3,500

On 1/31/05 he repays Rosenkrantz $3,000 principal and $100 interest expense on the previously recorded loan. The total payment to Rosenkrantz is $3,100. Clearly, cash decreases by $3,100. Also the principal on the note decreases by $3,000. But what about the $100 interest? This is an expense. So we have a decrease in an asset offset by a decrease in a liability and an increase in expense, which you will remember, is also a decrease in equity.

Date	Acct.#	Account Description	Debit	Credit
1/31/2005	210	Notes Payable	$3,000	
	510	Interest Expense	100	
	101	Cash in Bank		$3,100

This transaction could have been broken into two recorded transactions as follows:

Date	Acct.#	Account Description	Debit	Credit
1/31/2005	210	Notes Payable	$3,000	
	101	Cash in Bank		$3,000

Date	Acct.#	Account Description	Debit	Credit
1/31/2005	510	Interest Expense	$100	
	101	Cash in Bank		$100

There is no bar to having recorded transactions involve more than two accounts, as long as the total debits and credits in the entry are equal and the elements of the transaction are related to the same event.

These transactions have to be posted to the appropriate general ledger account. Here are the accounts after the postings:

Cash in Bank

5,000	1,500
15,000	9,100
8,000	3,500
	3,100
28,000	17,200

Service Fees

DR	CR
	8,000

Office Rent Expense

DR	CR
1,500	

Office Furniture

DR	CR
9,100	

Owners Equity

DR	CR
	5,000

Interest Expense

DR	CR
100	

Owners Draw

DR	CR
3,500	

Notes Payable

DR	CR
3,000	15,000

Summary

- Transactions should be recorded promptly in well-designed journals. Recorded information should include the date of the transaction, the parties involved, the dollar amounts disbursed or collected, and the nature of the transaction.
- Transactions recorded in journals must be transferred or posted to the appropriate general ledger accounts. Each such posting involves equal and offsetting changes in two accounts because such changes are always required to insure that the basic accounting equation (assets = liabilities + equity) is maintained.
- Each general ledger account is "T" shaped which provides a clear demarcation between the left and right side of the account. Asset accounts are always increased by postings on the left side of the "T" because they are on the left side of the fundamental equation. Liability and equity accounts are always increased by postings on the right side of the "T" because these accounts are on the right side of the fundamental equation. Decreases in accounts are posted on the opposite side of the "T" from increases.
- The term "debit" refers to the left side of every account; the term "credit" refers to the right side of every "T" account. That is all these terms mean in accounting. These terms are not synonymous with "increase" or "decrease" or "gain" or "loss".
- The key to properly posting transactions involves understanding what accounts are being changed and then applying the appropriate posting rules.

Exercises

1. Define the term *debit.*
2. Define the term *credit.*
3. To decrease an asset account, do you debit or credit the account?
4. To decrease a liability account, do you debit or credit the account?
5. To decrease an equity account, do you debit or credit the account?
6. To increase an asset account, do you debit or credit the account?
7. To increase a liability account, do you debit or credit the account?
8. To increase an income account, do you debit or credit the account?
9. To increase an expense account, do you debit or credit the account?

10. Give three examples of books of original entry used to record cash disbursements.
11. What are the most important elements of a cash disbursement transaction that need to be recorded?
12. Give three examples of books of original entry used to record cash receipts?
13. What is the posting process?
14. What is the relationship between the fundamental accounting equation and the procedure for increasing and decreasing various accounts?

Problem

1.Lilly Bopeep starts a sheep shearing service called "*Here's Looking at Ewe Kid*". Listed below are the transactions for her first month's operation. Record each transaction in general journal form. Set up T accounts and post the journalized transactions to the T accounts.

a.Lily deposits $5,000 of her own funds into a business checking account.
b.Lily purchases $1,000 of shearing equipment.
c.Lily keeps a cash disbursements journal. Column totals for the month indicate a total of $1,440 disbursements broken down as follows:

Expenses	$
Rent	500
Office Supplies	150
Advertising	275
Professional Services	125
Phone	95
Bank Charges	25
Postage	75
Insurance	110
Travel	85
Total	$ 1,440

d.Cash revenue consists of $2,000 of shearing revenue.
e.List the account balances indicating whether the account is a debit or credit balance.
f. Create a balance sheet and income statement.

Chapter 4

**Accounting can be
an *accrual* mistress.**

In This Chapter

- Cash versus Accrual
  Accounting

- Economic Reality and
  the Matching Concept

Bases of Accounting:
Timing is Everything

In the previous chapter we introduced the concept of transactions. Every example of a transaction included in that discussion involved increases or decreases in cash. Is it possible to accurately assess how a business performed if only cash transactions are recorded in the general ledger? The answer, to a certain extent, depends upon the nature of the business, but generally recording only cash exchanges will lead to problems in measuring economic performance. An example will illustrate these difficulties.

Example. Suppose you are the bookkeeper for *Joint Ventures*, the delivery business introduced in the last chapter. As bookkeeper you record all transactions based upon entries you find in the company's checkbook register for the month of December. Let's say the December checkbook has only two entries:

Date	Ck.#	Payee/Source	Deposit	Withdrawal	Balance
Beg.Bal.					10,000.00
Dec. 1	1010	Hurts Airplane Rental		(9,000.00)	1,000.00
Dec. 15	--	Columbian Growers Coop	5,000.00		6,000.00

Based on this register you record the two transactions in the general journal and then post to the appropriate accounts. The owner, Jimmy Morrisin, wants you to prepare an income statement for the month of December. Since there is only one income item and one expense item, your income statement will look like:

Joint Ventures
Cash Basis Income Statement
For Month Ended
December 31, 2004

Revenue	
Delivery Service	$ 5,000
Expenses	
Equipment Leases	9,000
Net Loss	$ (4,000)

Jimmy looks at this financial statement and says "bummer." Then he gazes intently at the statement and says "whoa man, you must be smoking too much of the product I deliver, because I had a way better month than your statement indicates. I mean, I did a $50,000 delivery for the *Columbian Growers Co-op*. The $5,000 deposit in December was just the up front fee. I made the delivery in late December, and they paid me the $45,000 balance at the beginning of January. But I **earned** the whole fee in December, because that's when I made the delivery."

"For another thing, that $9,000 payment to *Hurts* is for **three** months plane rental. Those mothers make me pay three months in **advance**. The way I figure, only $3,000 should count against December, and the rest should go against January and February."

"It seems to me, I really **earned** $47K rather than lost $4K."

You say sheepishly, "Look, I only went by the checkbook, and it says you took in only $5,000 in revenue and spent $9,000. Looking at cash, you were down $4,000 for the month. Besides it will all even out over a long enough period of time."

"Well, yeah," answers Jim. "I can see your point, but what if I want a more accurate picture of what actually happened in December? I'm interested in the long run. But I also want to know what happened in the most recent month because I want to respond quickly to any good or bad trends that might be showing up in the numbers. No offense, but that statement you gave me does not reflect what **really** happened in December."

Economic Reality and the Matching Concept

What does Jim mean by asking you for a more accurate picture? He intuitively knows there is a natural and logical causal relationship between revenue and the expenses it takes to generate that revenue. The attempt to capture this causal relationship between revenue and expense is called the **matching concept**. By this matching concept, Jim realized that he really earned $50,000 in fees in December and incurred only $3,000 in expenses. He knew that recording only the cash transactions distorted this economic reality.

Accrual Accounting

Because of the potential economic distortions caused by recording only cash transactions, GAAP requires that revenue and expenses should be recorded on an **accrual basis**. This means that a business records revenue when the earning process is complete, not necessarily when cash is received. For example, a tavern that allows customers to run a tab records revenue when the customer receives the drink, not when the tab is paid.

Similarly, using an accrual basis of accounting, expenses are recorded when the business receives the goods and services, not necessarily when the business actually pays for them. If a bar receives a supply of napkins but does not pay for them for thirty days, the expense is recognized when the napkins are delivered and used, not when the bill is paid.

Advantages and Disadvantages of Cash and Accrual Systems

A business that records revenue only when cash is received, and expenses only when they are paid is said to be on the **cash basis** of accounting. An obvious advantage of the cash basis system over the accrual system is that it is much simpler. An accrual system requires more accounts, including Accounts Receivable, Accounts Payable, Inventory, Prepaid Expenses, and Deferred Revenue. Each of these accrual accounts requires making estimates and sometimes complex computations. As in machinery the more moving parts the more potential problems.

The cash basis accounting approach requires no complex measurements or estimates. An expense is recognized only when a vendor is paid for a product or service. Revenue is recorded only when a customer or client pays for products sold or services rendered.

The disadvantage of the cash basis system is that for any particular short period of time operating results can be greatly distorted from economic reality. The distortions usually result from transactions occurring near the end of accounting periods.

Does Cash Basis Accounting Always Provide Different Operating Results From Accrual Accounting?

The answer is no. If most of a firm's sales are cash sales and most expenses are paid immediately, there is little difference between the measured operating results using a cash basis versus an accrual basis of accounting. However, if a business extends credit to customers, has credit extended to it, or carries significant amounts of inventory, the differences in reported operating results using the two approaches can be significant.

For many businesses, cash collections may lag behind earnings by two to three months. Payments on expenses may also lag as much as sixty days from the receipt of goods and services. In these cases cash basis earnings may greatly differ from accrual basis earnings.

Over the entire life cycle of a business, cumulative operating results are the same under both bases of accounting. In fact, year to year the differences may not be that great if the levels of revenue and expense remain stable and the collection and payment cycles do not fluctuate. The greatest variation between accrual and cash basis accounting tend to occur in the initial and ending periods of a firm's life cycle, or during periods of significant growth or decline. Short term monthly and quarterly reporting also can be greatly different. As our friend Jim indicated, accurate short term reporting is very important in managing a business.

In the following chapters we will consider in more detail the complexity associated with accrual accounting.

Summary

- There are two commonly used bases of accounting: cash basis and accrual basis.
- In cash basis accounting revenue is recognized only when cash is received from clients or customers. Expenses are recorded and recognized only when vendors are paid.
- In accrual accounting revenue is recognized when earned, not necessarily when cash is received. Expenses are recognized when incurred, not necessarily when cash is paid to vendors.

- Cash basis is a simpler system of accounting than accrual accounting but its use can sometimes significantly distort the reporting of economic performance.
- Accrual accounting is more complicated than cash basis accounting because it requires more accounts and the use of estimates. However, it does provide a more economically realistic assessment of economic performance because revenues and expenses are always matched to each other.

Exercises

1. Why is the cash basis of accounting simple to use?
2. What problems arise in using cash basis accounting?
3. State the matching concept.
4. What are the fundamental principles of accrual accounting?
5. How does accrual accounting conform to the matching concept?

Problem

1. Jane Jones opens a flight school she calls *Plane Jane Academy*. In December, her check register contains the following transactions:

Plane Jane's Check Register				
Date	Ck.#	Payee/Source	$	Balance
				750.00
Dec. 5	-	Tuition Deposit	1,500	2,250.00
Dec. 8	1005	Office Park	(400)	1,850.00

The $1,500 tuition deposit on December 5 is payment for five classes. One class will be given in December. The remaining four classes will not be taught until the following year. The check to Office Park is for December's rent. Prepare a cash basis income statement for December. Then prepare an accrual basis income statement. Which statement best reflects the performance of *Plane Jane Academy* in December?

Chapter 5

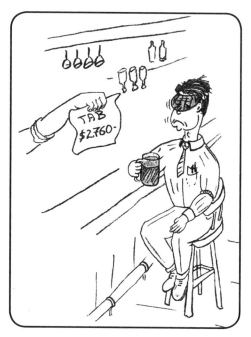

**Substance and credit abuse
often go hand-in-hand.**

In This Chapter

- Accounts Receivable
- Accounts Receivable
  Valuation Problems
- Accounts Payable
- Subsidiary Ledgers

Receivables & Payables: Promises, Promises

In accrual accounting, revenue is recorded when earned, and expenses recorded when incurred. A customer's obligation to pay for goods and services provided is called **accounts receivable**. From the firm's point of view, accounts receivable are assets. When a firm receives goods or services from another business before payment, the firm incurs a liability called **accounts payable**.

Accounts Receivable

When a business extends credit to customers, it assumes a certain risk that it may not be able to collect what it is owed. Why would a business be willing to let customers wait to pay for goods and services they have already received? Perhaps you have seen the sign over a business counter that says, " In God we trust...all others pay cash". Indeed, it would seem like a more prudent business practice to insist on cash payment as soon as goods or services are delivered. Or, even better why not get paid before goods and services are delivered?

Generally, firms extend credit to customers and clients because *they have to*. If a business refuses to extend credit it may lose customers to competitors who do. Many managers conclude that the additional revenue made by extending credit outweigh the costs of non-collection of receivables.

When a business extends credit to its customers, it records a revenue transaction at the time it provides its customer with goods or services. The transaction results in a revenue account increase and an increase in an asset account. Since no cash is received, the asset account that is increased is Accounts Receivable.

Example. When *Joint Ventures* made its December delivery for the *Columbian Grower's Co-op* they did not pay them the balance owed until January. When the delivery was completed the *Co-op* had an obligation to pay *Joint Ventures* for its services. *Joint Ventures* completed the $50,000 delivery on December 20. Recall that the *Co-op* had already paid $5,000 on the delivery, so on December 20 the following journal entry would be made:

Date	Acct.#	Account Description	Debit	Credit
12/20/2004	104	Accounts Receivable	$45,000	
	401	Revenue		$45,000

Accounts Receivable is an asset account. Notice that no cash account was involved in the transaction, because no cash changed hands. An asset account was increased and equity (revenue) was increased. If on January 5 the *Co-op* paid the $45,000 owed the transaction would be recorded in this way:

Date	Acct.#	Account Description	Debit	Credit
1/5/2005	101	Cash	$45,000	
	104	Accounts Receivable		$45,000

Notice that no revenue account was affected by the January payment. This is because the revenue was recorded in December 2004, when *Joint Ventures* actually earned it. In January, all that happened was that one asset account, Cash, increased, while another asset account, Accounts Receivable, decreased.

Valuation Problems and the Potential for Management Mischief

Sometimes customers fail to make good on what they owe. This failure to pay may be willful, but often it is not. Usually, customers intend to pay for the goods and services they acquire, but due to unforeseen economic setbacks or failure to adequately control spending, they find themselves unable to make payments. This very ordinary circumstance creates a valuation problem.

Let's say a firm has $15,000 of receivables at the end of an accounting period. Can the firm determine if these receivables are fully collectable? If the accounts receivable are not fully collectable, assets and revenue are overstated. Arriving at a reasonable valuation of accounts receivable usually is not that difficult, but getting a **precise** dollar amount of collectable accounts is not usually possible. Welcome to the world of accounting estimates!

A figure for accounts receivable on a balance sheet of a company with a large number of individual accounts reflects an estimate of what the company believes is collectable. You hope that the estimate is made in good faith and is reasonable. However, sometimes managers do not act in good faith, and they inflate the amount of receivables they deem to be collectable. This results in an overstatement of both assets and revenues.

The most common method of estimating the collectability of receivables is to use an *aging schedule*. In an aging schedule, accounts receivable are classified in terms of how long they have been outstanding. A typical schedule divides receivables into categories of less than 30 days, 31-60 days, 61-90 days, and over 90 days. Based on general credit experience, the longer a receivable is outstanding, the less the chance for full collection.

Example. Let's say that *Joint Ventures* accounts receivables total $75,000 at the end of the most recent year. Based on past credit experience Morrisin estimates that 90% of receivables under 30 days will be paid, 70% of those between 31-60 days will be paid, 60% of those between 61-90 days, will be paid and only 50% of those over 90 days will be paid. If the distribution of the $75,000 receivables is broken down in an aging schedule, *Joint Ventures* would estimate the collectable receivables as follows:

Joint Ventures Aging Schedule

Aging Category	Total	% Collectable	$ Collectable
<30 Days	$ 55,000	90%	$ 49,500
31-60 Days	10,000	70%	7,000
61-90 Days	6,000	60%	3,600
>90	4,000	50%	2,000
	$ 75,000		$ 62,100

Sometimes the valuation question may go beyond simply making a good faith estimate of collectability. In some situations management may be tempted to commit outright fraud. Because no cash is collected when sales are made "on account", a corrupt management can record fraudulent additional sales by simply creating fictitious customers and recording fictitious sales.

Another time honored-means of inflating Accounts Receivable and Sales Revenue involves what as known as "keeping the books open" at the end of the accounting period. In this case the customers and sales are real but January sales are recorded as December sales so the end of year financial statements include inflated assets and revenue.

Part of the audit function is to test the existence and collectability of accounts receivable and this can serve as a brake on such fraudulent practices. In the audit of large companies with millions of dollars of receivables and hundreds of thousands of individual accounts the audit process relies on statistical sampling, which usually provides a reasonable, but not exact, estimate of collectable accounts.

Accounts Payable

Just as a business extends credit to its customers, other firms may extend credit to it. When a business receives goods or services but does not pay immediately, it incurs a liability called **accounts payable**. Using an accrual basis of accounting a business records the purchase of goods or services in the period when they are used, not necessarily when cash is paid.

Example. Say that *Joint Ventures* was granted credit by an office supply store to purchase $600 of office supplies at the end of December 2004. *Joint Ventures* received and used the office supplies in that month. *Joint Ventures* actually paid for the supplies in January 2005. The entry at the date of purchase is:

Date	Acct.#	Account Description	Debit	Credit
12/15/2004	510	Office Supplies Expense	$ 600	
	201	Accounts Payable		$600

Office Supplies, an expense account, has increased while a liability account, Accounts Payable, has also increased. Remember, when an expense is incurred equity decreases. What actually happens is that a liability account increases and an equity account decreases, so the fundamental accounting equation is maintained.

When *Joint Ventures* pays cash for what it owes in January 2005, the following entry is made:

Date	Acct.#	Account Description	Debit	Credit
1/15/2005	201	Accounts Payable	$ 600	
	101	Cash		$600

In this transaction a decrease in an asset (Cash), is offset by a decrease in a liability (Accounts Payable). No expense is recognized in 2005 because the supplies were used in 2004. The net effect of these two transactions is that *Joint Ventures* recognized the expense when it used the supplies, rather than when it actually paid for them.

Potential Management Mischief

Management may have a motive to understate payables, as this understates expenses and overstates net income. Usually the amount of payable understatement is not too **material** and such understatement can easily be detected. What is a *material understatement*? A small or insignificant dollar amount. Generally auditors and accountants define materiality based upon a small percentage of total assets or total revenue.

Subsidiary Ledgers

If a business only has credit sales (i.e., it never receives cash when the sale is made), all cash collections from customers can be deemed to be credits to Accounts Receivable. Conversely if a business has no credit sales (i.e., it never extends credit and receives cash whenever the sale is made), all cash received from customers can be credited to a revenue account.

A good number of businesses fall between these extremes. Sometimes they extend credit and sometimes they receive cash immediately. To avoid accounting confusion and accurately track accounts receivable, a business that extends credit to customers must maintain a special set of accounting records called **subsidiary ledgers**. An accounts receivable subsidiary ledger consists of the revenue and payment history of each customer to which a business extends credit.

Example. Assume that the *Columbian Growers Co-op* contracts with *Joint Ventures* for three deliveries and makes two payments in 2005. The accounts receivable subsidiary ledger on *Joint Ventures* would look like this:

Joint Ventures Accounts Receivable Subsidiary Ledger			
Customer : Columbian Growers Coop			
	Dr	Cr	Balance
3/15 Delivery	50,000		50,000
4/18 Payment		50,000	-
7/21 Delivery	25,000		25,000
9/05 Payment		25,000	-
12/01 Delivery	30,000		30,000

In a manual accounting system, a business like *Joint Ventures* has to record all deliveries and payments twice: once in the general journal, and once again in the subsidiary ledger. Because two postings are required for each delivery and payment, transcription errors may cause the ending balance of the accounts receivable to not agree to the cumulative ending balances in the subsidiary ledgers. Finding such discrepancies can be a time consuming and expensive process.

When using computerized accounting software, all payments and deliveries are posted simultaneously to the subsidiary ledger and the general ledger Accounts Receivable account. In fact, in a computerized software system even customers who pay cash at the time of the sale have such transactions recorded in the general ledger and subsidiary ledger *as if it were a credit transaction*. In this case, the service or product delivery date is the same as the payment date.

Summary

- When a business sells a product or delivers a service and allows a customer to defer payment until a later date it has extended credit to that customer.
- When a business receives a product or service and is granted the right to defer payment to the vendor it has been extended credit.

- Under the accrual accounting method a business extending credit to its customers recognizes and records an asset, accounts receivable, and an increase in revenue at the time of sale or delivery of service.
- Under the accrual accounting method a business that is extended credit recognizes and records a liability, accounts payable, and an increase in expense at the time the vendor provides goods or services.
- Subsequent cash receipts from customers reduce accounts receivable. Subsequent payments to vendors reduce accounts payable.
- Because customers do not always repay amounts owed, accountants and management must make an estimate of what percentage of total accounts receivable is actually collectable.
- The presence of accounts receivable increases the record keeping burden and provides opportunities for fraudulent overstatement of assets and revenue.

Exercises

1. When a business provides goods or services before receiving cash payment, what type of asset is created?
2. When a business receives goods or services before paying cash for them, what sort of liability is created?
3. What risks are associated with a business extending credit to its customers?
4. What risks are associated with a business not extending credit to its customers?
5. When a business makes a sale but does not receive cash immediately what accounts are debited and credited? When cash payment is later made, what accounts are debited and credited?
6. When a business purchases an item on credit what types of accounts are debited and credited? When cash payment is later made what accounts are debited and credited?
7. Describe two ways management can fraudulently increase revenue utilizing accounts receivable accounts.
8. What method is commonly used to estimate the collectability of accounts receivable?
9. Do some brief research on the question of consumer credit and its role in the economy. Are credit policies too lax? Have overall credit levels increased or decreased in recent years? What is the relationship between personal bankruptcies and consumer credit?

Problem

1. Denise Divine operates the *What a Drag Costume Company*. She extends credit to one of her biggest customers, a Mr. Crossley Dresser. The following "transactions" take place in December 2004 and January 2005. Assume that Crossley had no balance due at the beginning of December.

   a. December 6. Crossley rents a costume for four days at a rental price of $200. The fee is not paid at the time, but is "on account."
   b. December 15. Crossley rents another costume for a week, with a rental price of $250. This was also "on account."
   c. December 26. Crossley rents another costume for two weeks with a rental price of $400.
   d. January 15, 2005. Crossley pays his entire balance due of $850.

Set up a subsidiary accounts receivable ledger for Mr. Dresser. Record the above transactions in this ledger and in the general journal. What portion, if any, of the December 26 rental should be reflected as December revenue, as opposed to January revenue?

Chapter 6

**Prepayment requirements can
impede the "flow" of commerce.**

In This Chapter

- Deferred Revenue
- Prepaid Expenses

Cash First, Goods or Services Later

A business that provides goods or services before it collects cash recognizes accounts receivable. Some businesses are in the fortunate position to be able to demand cash payments in advance of providing goods or services. For example, building lessors typically require a month's rent in advance, and insurance companies collect cash premiums covering a year in advance.

In accrual accounting a business receiving payments in advance incurs a liability called **deferred revenue** at the time of cash collection. This liability is the obligation to provide the goods or services that are already paid for. The obligation is discharged and revenue recognized only after the business delivers the good or services.

If a business pays for goods or services before they are actually delivered, an asset called **prepaid expense** is recorded when payment is made. An actual expense is recognized and recorded only after the goods or services are delivered.

Example. Recall *Joint Ventures* had to pay *Hurt's Plane Rental* $9,000 in December 2004 in advance for a three-month plane lease. If a cash basis of accounting is used, all $9,000 is recognized as a December expense. Using an accrual basis of accounting better reflects economic reality because only $3,000 will be recognized as December expense. The other $6,000 will be recognized as expenses in January and February of the following year. When *Joint Ventures* pays *Hurt's* $9,000 on December 1 the transaction is recorded like this:

Date	Acct.#	Account Description	Debit	Credit
12/1/2004	105	Prepaid Expenses	$9,000	
	101	Cash in Bank		$9,000

An asset, Prepaid Expenses, is increased and another asset, Cash in Bank, is decreased.

Assuming *Hurt's Plane Rental* utilizes an accrual basis of accounting, they record a liability when they receive *Joint Ventures* payment. On their books the transaction looks like this:

Date	Acct.#	Account Description	Debit	Credit
12/1/2004	101	Cash in Bank	$9,000	
	220	Deferred Revenue		$9,000

A liability is recognized by *Hurt's* because as of December 1 it still has to deliver three months worth of plane use to *Joint Ventures*. The key point is that *Hurt's* does not recognize revenue, nor does *Joint Ventures* recognize expense at the time cash changes hands. Only after an actual service is delivered is revenue and expense recognized. When does this happen?

In this situation the service in question is the leasing of a plane. At the end of December *Joint Ventures* will have had one month's use of the plane. So at the end of December the following entry on *Joint Ventures'* books is made to reflect the rental expense for that month:

Date	Acct.#	Account Description	Debit	Credit
12/31/2004	505	Plane Rental Expense	$3,000	
	105	Prepaid Expenses		$3,000

Notice that the Rental Expense account for the month would have a $3,000 debit balance and the Prepaid Expense account would have a $6,000 balance. In January and February of 2005 similar entries have to be made to properly reflect the correct plane rental expense for these months.

At the end of December the following entry is made in *Hurts'* books:

Date	Acct.#	Account Description	Debit	Credit
12/31/2004	220	Deferred Revenue	$3,000	
	400	Rental Revenue		$3,000

Again, similar entries will be made at the end of January and February.

Management Mischief with Deferred Revenue and Prepaid Expenses

A manager can overstate income and understate liabilities by treating deferred revenue as earned revenue. Essentially, this shady practice seeks to recognize revenue before it is actually earned. Such mischief often is not easy to detect, because it is not always clear when the earnings process is fully complete.

A manager also can understate current year expenses by claiming they are prepaid expenses. This amounts to a fraudulent claim that payments for a certain service benefit future accounting periods when, in fact, they do not. Recently a large telecommunications company incurred significant cash expenses on maintenance of its utility lines. It fraudulently classified most of the outlays as prepaid expense rather than current period expense. Since prepaid expenses are recorded as an asset rather than an expense, expenses were understated; and hence, profits were overstated.

Summary

- In accrual accounting, the payment of cash for goods and services that will be delivered at some later point is recorded as an asset, prepaid expense. The expense is not recorded until the goods or services are actually utilized.
- In accrual accounting, the collection of cash from customers before goods or services are delivered is recorded as a liability, deferred revenue. Revenue is not recorded until goods or services are actually delivered to the customer.

Exercises

1. Define a prepaid expense and give at least two examples.
2. Define deferred revenue. Give two examples.
3. Attorneys frequently demand and receive cash before they provide significant legal services. This form of deferred revenue is sometimes called a *retainer*. What is the economic justification for prepaying lawyers?

Problem

1. The *Good Intentions Road Paving Company* retains Attorney Steve Churnam to defend the company in a lawsuit bought by the Town of Gehenna. The *Company* resurfaced the main street of the town, Soon after the town paid the *Company*, the road surface began to crack. The town is suing the *Company* for using inadequate paving materials. Attorney Churnam and the *Company* engage in the following transactions:

> a. On December 10, 2005, before proceeding with any work the *Company* pays Churnam a retainer of $10,000.
>
> b. After doing 40 hours of work on the case Churnam, charges the *Company* $10,000. Since Churnam has already received $10,000 the *Company* is not billed for this work. However, Churnam expects to work another 20 hours on the case so on December 28, 2004, he requests another $5,000 retainer from the *Company*.
>
> c. On January 12, 2005, the *Company* pays the additional $5,000 retainer.
>
> d. After Churnum works an additional 16 hours the *Company* settles the lawsuit with the town on February 5, 2005. Since the fee was only $4,000, Churnam writes a check to the *Company* for $1,000.

Record the journal transactions for the *Company* and for Churnam.

Chapter 7

**Some assets are more fixed
than others.**

In This Chapter

- Depreciation Expense
- Useful Lives of Fixed Assets
- The Historical Cost Principle

Fixed Assets and Depreciation Methods:
The Hysterical Cost Principle

You may recall that Jim, the owner of *Joint Ventures*, was less than thrilled with the need to lease a plane from *Hurt's Plane Rental*. So he decided to buy a used plane for $75,000.
How should the payment be recorded?

Since the expenditure is very large and the plane should be useful for several years, it is not reasonable to treat the acquisition as an expense. Clearly, the plane is an asset. Because the plane will help generate revenue over several periods, it is not a current period expense. The matching principle dictates that the cost of the asset ought to be spread over the number of periods that it will help generate revenue. This is the entry for the acquisition:

Date	Acct.#	Account Description	Debit	Credit
2/21/2005	150	Equipment	$75,000	
	101	Cash in Bank		$75,000

One asset account, Equipment, has increased while a second asset account, Cash, has decreased.

Notice that no expense has been recognized. Notice also that *Joint Ventures* will no longer be leasing planes. If no other entries are made, no expense will be recognized in association with the use of an aircraft. This, of course, would not make economic sense, because to make deliveries a plane is needed. Also, the plane has a limited useful life, so at some point it will run down and need to be replaced.

From both a physical and economic standpoint, the value of *Joint Ventures'* plane declines over time and use. The decline in an asset's economic and physical value is called **depreciation**. According to GAAP, depreciation is an expense that must be periodically reflected on *Joint Ventures'* books. Recording depreciation is the way in which an asset's economic benefits are allocated over its useful life.

The tricky issues in recording depreciation are estimating the asset's useful life and choosing an appropriate rate of depreciation. Welcome, once again, to the world of accounting estimates. Equipment manufacturers often give estimates of the range of expected useful lives of their equipment, subject to variations in maintenance and operating conditions. Management must choose a realistic assessment of an asset's useful life from this range.

Estimating an asset's useful life solves half of the depreciation question. What about the rate of depreciation? Will the physical deterioration of equipment occur evenly over its useful life? Or will the decline be more rapid at the beginning or end of an asset's useful life? Should depreciation be based on the decline in an asset's economic value instead of its physical deterioration? The two forms of decline do not necessarily occur simultaneously. For example, the market value of computers declines very rapidly compared to their physical deterioration.

Because there is wide variation in the physical and economic characteristics of assets, GAAP sanctions several depreciation methods. The **straight-line method** divides the purchase price of the asset by the expected useful life. If an asset is expected to rapidly decline, an **accelerated method** can be used.

Example. Assume that *Joint Venture's* plane will last twenty years. There is no reason to assume that this plane will physically deteriorate more rapidly in the beginning or end of its useful life, so the straight-line method is used. Dividing $75,000 by 20 years gives an annual depreciation amount $3,750 per year. The entry for recording the annual depreciation is:

Date	Acct.#	Account Description	Debit	Credit
12/31/2005	521	Depreciaton Expense	$3,750	
	151	Accumulated Depreciation		$3,750

Accumulated depreciation is known as a *contra asset* account. It is found on the left (asset) side of the balance sheet, but unlike other assets, it normally has a credit balance. The idea is to allow an asset's acquisition price to be reflected at its original cost, offset by the amount of depreciation taken against it.

The fixed asset section of *Joint Venture's* balance sheet as of 12/31/05 would look like this:

Fixed Assets	
Plane	$ 75,000
Accumulated Depreciation	(3,750)
Net Fixed Assets	$ 71,250

Because businesses usually have several fixed assets purchased at different times, with different useful lives and different depreciation methods, it is necessary to keep a separate schedule of these assets called a **fixed asset schedule**. Here is an example of a portion of a fixed asset schedule :

			Joint Ventures Fixed Asset Schedule				
Asset Number	Description	Date Acquired	Cost	Method	Useful Life	Prior Depreciation	12/31/2005 Depreciation
1	Airplane	1/21/2005	75,000	S/L	20	-	3,750
2	UZIs	2/12/2005	2,500	DDB	5	-	1,000
3	Radar Jammer	2/15/2005	12,500	S/L	10	-	1,250

The Hysterical Cost Principle

Under GAAP rules, asset acquisitions are initially recorded at their original cost. Although an allowance for depreciation is reflected against most assets, no attempt is made to adjust these historical costs to current market values. This is called the **historical cost principle**.

The failure to adjust fixed assets for changes in market value may, to a certain extent, impair the usefulness of the balance sheet. Recall that the balance sheet attempts to reflect the financial condition of the business by listing the **values** of the firm's assets, liabilities and equity at the end of the accounting period. Most readers of the balance sheet would hope that the values reflected are at least close to current market values. Current market value is the amount that would be realized if the asset were sold. If the values associated with various fixed assets do not reflect current market values, the balance sheet provides a less than accurate portrayal of economic condition.

The extent of the balance sheet distortion caused by the historical cost principle depends upon the nature of a firm's asset holdings. If the business does not hold many fixed assets or the net depreciated values do not diverge too much from current market values there is not too much of a problem. However significant distortions can occur if a business owns a significant amount of real estate.   Land, for example, is never depreciated. However, its current value is likely to deviate significantly from its historical acquisition price. Improved real estate such as office buildings and warehouses, are depreciated, but their current market values may actually increase over time. So if a business owns significant amounts of real property, the historical cost principle can significantly distort the portrayal of economic condition.

GAAP does not allow the adjustment of fixed assets, such as real estate, to current market values primarily because managers would constantly be tempted to overstate the value of their fixed assets to improve the appearance of their firm's economic condition. In effect, the historical cost principle is applied because accountants believe that distortions of economic condition that involve understatement of asset values are preferable to distortions caused by overstated values.

Example. *The Chump Realty Group* constructed a luxury apartment complex, *Le Brut Pompidour*, at a cost of $36,000,000 in 1995. The cost includes $3,000,000 for acquisition of the land. The remaining $33,000,000 associated with the construction was subject to straight-line depreciation over 30 years. For each year through 2004 depreciation expense was recognized at $1,100,000 per year. At the end of 2004 *Chump's* balance sheet reflects the project in this way:

Apartment Complex, at cost	$	33,000,000
Less accumulated depreciation		(11,000,000)
		22,000,000
Land		3,000,000
	$	25,000,000

A recent appraisal shows the fair market value of the complex to be $65,000,000. Assuming this appraisal is realistic, the difference between the historical cost of the asset reported on the balance sheet and its fair market value is $40,000,000!

Management Mischief

Because GAAP allows so many different methods of depreciation and the useful life of assets is subject to varying estimates, there is plenty of opportunity for management mischief. Management can make a firm appear more profitable than it really is by understating depreciation expense by overstating the useful life of assets. It also can keep obsolete and no longer used assets on the balance sheet, simply to avoid recording a loss on the disposal of the assets.

Summary

- An expenditure for an asset that will help a firm generate revenue for more than one year should not be treated as an expense of the year in which it is acquired. Instead, the cost of the asset is spread over its expected useful life and recorded annually as *depreciation expense*.
- When recording depreciation expense, a *contra asset account*, called *Accumulated Depreciation* is credited. Accumulated Depreciation is shown on the balance sheet as an offset to an asset's original acquisition cost.
- The historical cost principle does not allow fixed assets to be periodically adjusted to current market values. This may lead to some distortion of economic condition reported on the balance sheets of companies whose assets have appreciated in value, such as those that own a significant amount of real property.

Exercises.

1. Explain the concept of depreciation. How does it relate to the matching concept?
2. What is the historical cost principle?
3. Why does GAAP not allow the upward adjustment of fixed assets like building and land to fair market values?
4. Which two accounts are used to record depreciation expense?

Problems

1. The *Slippery Slope Rock Climbing Supply Company* has just purchased the following items:
    a. A computer for $2,500 which should last for five years.
    b. A piece of land for rock climbing classes for $20,000.
    c. Display cases and office furniture for $14,000, which should last for seven years.
    d. A $25 first aid kit that should last for a year.

Which of the above items should be subject to depreciation? Assuming straight-line depreciation, compute and record in journal format the annual depreciation entries.

Chapter 8

Who says accountants are not "keen" on art?

In This Chapter

- Inventory

- Gross Profit

- Cost of Goods Sold

- Inventory Flow Assumptions

- Perpetual and Periodic Bookkeeping for Inventory

- Lower of Cost or Market Rule

Inventory and Costs of Goods Sold:
Moving the Merch

Some businesses sell products, like shoe stores, others sell services, like chiropodists. Goods sold to customers are assets called *inventory*. Inventory measurements can be surprisingly difficult. Different inventory measurement approaches can lead to wide variations in reported profits or losses.

Buy Low, Sell High

The difference between a product's sale price and its cost is called the *gross margin* or *gross profit*. Obviously, the higher the margin, the better. The cost of the product is called *cost of goods sold*. We would hope that computing gross profit would involve a simple subtraction of total cost of goods sold from total sales. Alas, things turn out to be more complicated.

Adding total sales generally poses no great measurement problem, but calculating the cost of goods sold is not as straightforward. The basic difficulty arises when a business does not completely sell all its goods during the accounting period. In fact, most firms finish their year with unsold inventory. Valuing the unsold year end inventory is the primary source of complexity in figuring out the cost of goods sold.

Example. Janis buys and sells a silicon gel compound used in the production of cosmetic surgery implants. Assume that Janis can sell an ounce of compound for $500 that costs her $250. Let's say Janis bought and sold precisely 100 ounces of compound during the year. What is her gross profit?

Janis' Gross Profit	
Sales	$ 50,000
Cost of Goods Sold	25,000
Gross Profit	$ 25,000

Now change the scenario and assume she bought 150 ounces of compound, but sold only 100 ounces during 2004. This means she has 50 ounces left at the end of the year. What is her gross profit now?

Janis' Incorrect Gross Profit	
Sales	$ 50,000
Cost of Goods Sold	37,500
Gross Profit	$ 12,500

The $37,500 cost of goods sold is derived by multiplying 150 times $250. But this does not make sense because unsold product on hand at the end of the year should not be treated as an expense. Treating unsold year-end inventory as an expense violates the matching concept and common sense. Instead, we need to complicate the computation of the cost of goods sold by taking into account ending inventory as follows:

Cost of Goods Sold = Beginning Inventory + Purchases - Ending Inventory

What would Janis' cost of goods sold look like assuming she had no beginning inventory, using the above formula?

Janis' Correct Cost of Goods Sold	
Beginning Inventory	$ 0
Purchases	37,500
Less: ending inventory	(12,500)
Cost of Goods Sold	$ 25,000

This matches our original cost of goods sold figure. To arrive at the $12,500 ending inventory figure, the 50 unsold ounces was multiplied by the purchase price of $250 per ounce. In this example, all Janis' purchases were made at the same price, $250 per ounce. In the real world, the per ounce cost is likely to fluctuate. Also, Janis, like many businesses, may offer more than one type of product with fluctuating prices. In order to accurately compute the cost of goods sold, Janis has to be able to get an accurate count of unsold inventory on hand and she also has to assign the "correct" costs to these products.

In assigning a cost to unsold inventory you would expect to use its *actual* cost. This is not as easy as you would think. For Janis to use the actual cost paid she must be able to identify the cost associated with the batches of product on hand at the end of the period. However, these batches might come from more than one purchase, each with a different purchase price.

Assume Janis stores her purchases in one big tank. Also assume that purchase prices fluctuated during the year. Because she keeps her product in one tank she cannot physically tell which batches go with which costs. She can certainly weigh the amount of product she has on hand at the end of the year, but how does she know the unit price to assign to her ending inventory?

In order to assign a cost to her ending inventory Janis will have to make *assumptions* about the flow of product in and out of her tank. One plausible flow assumption is called **FIFO**, standing for *first in, first out*. Under this assumption ending inventory is associated with costs from the most recent deliveries. An alternative flow assumption is called **LIFO**, standing for *last in, first out*. Under this flow assumption, ending inventory is associated with the oldest purchase costs. Alternatively, Janis might avoid making any flow assumption by simply using the **weighted average cost** of deliveries to value ending inventory.

The Effect of Different Flow Assumptions on Reported Gross Profit

You may think the choice of flow assumptions in assigning costs to ending inventory is a relatively minor issue. However, **the choice of inventory flow assumption can dramatically affect reported cost of goods sold, gross profit, and net income.**

Example. Assume that Janis received four shipments during the year as follows:

Janis' Product Purchases			
DATE	OUNCES	PRICE PER OUNCE	EXTENDED COST
Jan 5	40	$ 152.50	$ 6,100
Mar 15	30	180.00	5,400
Aug 25	40	300.00	12,000
Nov 12	40	350.00	14,000
	150		$ 37,500

If she has 50 ounces of compound unsold at the end of the year, different flow assumptions will yield different ending inventory figures. If she uses a **FIFO** approach, she will assume that the remaining inventory comes from the two most recent purchases:

FIFO Assumption for Ending Inventory

DATE	OUNCES	COST PER OUNCE	EXTENDED COST
Aug 25	10	$ 300.00	$ 3,000
Nov 12	40	350.00	14,000
		Ending Inventory Value	$ 17,000

If she uses a **LIFO** approach, she will assume that the remaining inventory derives from the oldest two purchases:

LIFO Assumption for Ending Inventory

DATE	OUNCES	COST PER OUNCE	EXTENDED COST
Jan 5	40	$ 152.50	$ 6,100
Mar 15	10	180.00	1,800
		Ending Inventory Value	$ 7,900

Alternatively, Janis could use a weighted average cost approach:

Weighted Average Approach

Total Purchases in Dollars:	$ 37,500
Total Purchases in Ounces:	150
Average Cost per Ounce (37,500/150):	$250
Production on hand in ounces:	50
Ending Inventory Value	$ 12,500

You can see that the three different approaches lead to a range of $7,900-17,000 in ending inventory value. The following table shows the variation in computed gross profit:

Janis' Gross Profit Using Different Inventory Flow Assumptions

	FIFO	Weighted Average	LIFO
Sales	$50,000	$50,000	$50,000
Cost of Goods Sold			
Beginning Inventory	0	0	0
Purchases	37,500	37,500	37,500
Less Ending Inventory	(17,000)	(12,500)	(7,900)
Cost of Goods Sold	20,500	25,000	29,600
Gross Profit in Dollars	$29,500	$25,000	$20,400
Gross Profit in Percentage	59%	50%	41%

Because the example uses relatively small dollar amounts, the dollar variation in gross profits under the different flow assumptions may not seem extreme. The gross profit percentages reveal more startling differences. Gross profit is reported as 59% of sales using **FIFO**, but only 41% of sales using **LIFO**. If you are looking at a company with millions in sales you can see just how dramatic an impact inventory flow assumptions can have on reported earnings.

GAAP: Do Your Own Thing

Does GAAP stipulate the specific flow assumption a business has to use? Actually, GAAP allows a business to use any flow assumptions it chooses, as long as it does so on a consistent basis. This means that the flow assumption used in one year must be used in the next.

Allowing different inventory flow assumptions means that two businesses with identical operating results can report dramatically different amounts of profit. To avoid this possibility, GAAP would have to require that all firms use the same inventory flow assumptions. Alternatively, GAAP could insist that all firms use a weighted average method of costing ending inventory.

As desirable as it would be for GAAP to reduce the number of acceptable, but widely divergent inventory flow assumptions, this is not likely to happen any time soon. This means that financial statement users have to be aware of the effect of these flow assumptions in comparing one firm's performance to another firm's. Fortunately, GAAP does require that firms disclose in their financial statements the inventory flow assumption used in computing cost of goods sold.

Two Methods of Bookkeeping for Inventories: Perpetual and Periodic

Two different methods are used for recording inventory transactions. Both methods lead to the same results, so the choice mainly depends upon the sophistication of the firm's accounting system. In the *perpetual method,* all inventory acquisitions are recorded as asset purchases. The cost of goods sold is not recorded until the inventory is actually sold.

This method requires that the business track the specific physical inventory flow from acquisition to sale. This is easy if the business has a relatively modest amount of discrete inventory. It is more difficult if there are large amounts of inventory or if the inventory is fungible.

Example. Assume that Janis purchases for cash 70 ounces of compound at $250 per ounce on February 15 and sells 30 ounces for $500 an ounce on February 28. This is the entry for the acquisition under the perpetual method:

Date	Acct.#	Account Description	Debit	Credit
2/15/2005	115	Inventory	$17,500	
	101	Cash in Bank		$17,500

An asset account, inventory, is increased, while another asset, cash, is decreased. Under the perpetual method of accounting, two entries need to be made when Janis sells 30 ounces of product. The recording of the sale is straightforward:

Date	Acct.#	Account Description	Debit	Credit
2/28/2005	101	Cash in Bank	$15,000	
	402	Sales		$15,000

Next the cost of the product sold needs to be recorded.

Date	Acct.#	Account Description	Debit	Credit
2/28/2005	420	Cost of Goods Sold	$7,500	
	115	Inventory		$7,500

An expense (a reduction in equity) is increased, while an asset is decreased.

The alternative to the perpetual recording system is the *periodic method.* Using this approach inventory purchases are first recorded as an expense. At the end of the accounting period, inventory on hand is counted and an adjustment is made to reflect this ending inventory as an asset.

When Janis purchased her initial product the entry using the periodic method would be:

Date	Acct.#	Account Description	Debit	Credit
2/15/2005	420	Cost of Goods Sold	$17,500	
	101	Cash in Bank		$17,500

When Janis sells her product in February no adjustment to inventory or cost of goods sold is made. So the sale entry is simply the same as the first half of the sale entry used in the perpetual method:

Date	Acct.#	Account Description	Debit	Credit
2/28/2005	101	Cash in Bank	$15,000	
	402	Sales		$15,000

In order to properly reflect the correct ending inventory at the end of February and reflect the correct cost of goods sold for the period, the following entry is made:

Date	Acct.#	Account Description	Debit	Credit
2/28/2005	115	Inventory	$10,000	
	420	Cost of Goods Sold		$10,000

The correct inventory figure is the amount on hand times the purchase price. Assuming that no one dipped into the inventory Janis should have 40 ounces of compound on hand at the end of the month, since she purchased 70 ounces and sold 30 ounces. This last entry insures that the amount of inventory and cost of goods sold is properly reflected.

Notice that under both methods the cost of goods sold and ending inventory amount are the same. Ending inventory is $10,000 and cost of goods sold is $7,500.

The Need for Physical Inventory Counts

Businesses that use the periodic method of recording inventory do not generally have an accounting system in place that can accurately track the flow of inventory. To accurately reflect the cost of goods sold and ending inventory at the end of the accounting period, such firms need to perform an accurate count of inventory on hand. Performing such a count can be expensive and time consuming, but is indispensable in arriving at an accurate accounting of cost of goods sold.

You might think that businesses with the ability to maintain a perpetual record of inventory would be able to dispense with the time consuming and expensive end of period physical counts of ending inventory. Think again. Tracking inventory on a perpetual and continuing basis entails faithfully increasing the inventory account when purchases are made, and decreasing the account when inventory is sold. In the real world stuff happens. Customers shoplift goods off the shelf. Employees help themselves to product or products become spoiled or damaged.

Balance Sheet Valuation Issues and the Lower of Cost or Market Rule

Ending inventory is recorded and reported at its cost. This means that inventory reported on the balance sheet does not reflect its retail value. Does the failure to reflect the current retail value of inventory lead to a distorted view of a firm's economic condition?

A similar question was raised about the failure to reflect on the balance sheet the current market value of real estate a company owns. However, the situation is not exactly analogous. Real estate usually comes in large bundles, while inventory comes in much smaller packets. It is very feasible to sell all real estate holdings in a handful of transactions, but selling all of a company's inventory would not be as simple. Selling inventory generally requires engaging in many, many small transactions. These transactions create costs. In fact, selling a company's entire inventory in bulk would almost certainly require giving the purchaser a large discount.

For this reason the failure to adjust ending inventory to fair market value does not distort the economic condition of a company to the degree that the failure to adjust real estate holdings does.

There is one circumstance in which GAAP requires a firm to adjust its inventory to its fair market value. GAAP requires that inventory must be carried on the books and reflected on the balance sheet at the **lower of cost or market value**. This means that inventory cannot be adjusted up to fair market value, but must be adjusted down when its fair market value declines below its cost.

When would the market value of inventory drop below its cost? Obsolescence, spoilage, changes in customer preferences, or dumb production and purchasing decisions are the usual culprits. If a business failed to adjust the carrying value of its inventory downward in such circumstances, its economic condition reflected on the balance sheet definitely would be distorted. In this case, the distortion would result in overstating a company's value, rather than understating it.

Mischief, Mischief, Mischief

Inventory offers a big opportunity for management to air brush their financial statements. If they want gross profits, and hence operating profits, to appear higher, the value of ending inventory simply needs to be overstated. There are many ways this can be done. The ending inventory value can be fudged upward by overstating the amount of inventory on hand. Unit costs assigned to ending inventory can be inflated as well. Or obsolete or damaged inventory can be included in the ending inventory count.

Sometimes for income tax purposes, management may want to show *lower* gross and operating profits. Ending inventory mis-measurement can be used for this purpose as well. In this situation, management seeks to undercount and undervalue ending inventory.

Summary

- Goods sold to customers are inventory.
- Gross Profit = Sales- Cost of Goods Sold.
- Cost of Goods Sold = beginning inventory + purchases- ending inventory.
- The determination of ending inventory value in computing cost of goods sold often requires making assumptions about the physical flow of goods through the business.
- Two widely used assumptions are FIFO and LIFO; first in first out, and last in first out. In lieu of a flow assumption, a weighted average approach can be used to value ending inventory.
- Different valuation methods can lead to dramatic differences in cost of goods sold.
- GAAP gives firms a choice of which flow assumption to use, but they must apply the chosen method consistently and disclose the method used.
- Inventories must be reported at cost, not retail value. The lower of cost or market rule specifies that previously recorded inventory must be adjusted downward if its market value falls below its original cost.

Exercises

1. Define the term "inventory".
2. What is gross profit?
3. What is the formula for computing costs of goods sold?
4. Why is there an adjustment made for ending inventory in computing current period costs of goods sold?
5. What are the two components of the ending inventory measurement?
6. Name the three basic inventory flow assumptions.
7. A direct relationship between two quantities exists when one quantity increases as the other increases, and vice versa. An inverse relationship exists between two quantities if one quantity increases as the other decreases and vice versa. Using these definitions specify whether the relationship between the following quantities is direct or inverse:
   a. Ending Inventory, Cost of Goods Sold.
   b. Beginning Inventory, Cost of Goods Sold
   c. Current Purchases, Cost of Goods Sold

    d. Ending Inventory, Gross Profit
    e. Gross Profit, Net Income
    f. Cost of Goods Sold, Gross Profit

8. Name three ways management can fraudulently inflate ending inventory?
9. Why would management wish to understate the value of ending inventory on its tax return?
10. What is the lower of cost or market rule?
11. Why are accurate end of period physical inventory counts needed using either the periodic or perpetual method of recording inventory?

Problems

1. The *Procrustean Bed Company* is a retailer of waterbeds (in only one size).   In February, they sold 40 beds for a total of $20,000. There was no beginning inventory, and during the month they had the following purchases from the manufacturer:

Bed Purchases

Date	Units	Unit Price	Cost
5-Feb	10	250	2,500
10-Feb	15	245	3,675
20-Feb	10	275	2,750
26-Feb	15	290	4,350
			13,275

Compute the cost of goods sold and gross profit under FIFO, LIFO and Average Cost flow assumptions.

2. Refer to problem 1 regarding the *Procrustean Bed Company*. Assume that the company had the following sales of beds in the month of February:

Date	Units Sold	Unit Price	Total Revenue
6-Feb	10	500	5,000
27-Feb	30	500	15,000
			20,000

Record the purchase and sale transactions in journal form first using the periodic method and then the perpetual method.

Chapter 9

Experts know how to choose the right tool for the job.

In This Chapter

- Adjusting Journal Entries
- Closing Entries
- Financial Statement Preparation

Adjusting and Closing the Books and Compiling Financial Statements: Pass the Eraser Please

Account balances sitting in general ledger "T" accounts do not provide a very useful format for accessing accounting information. Periodically, accountants need to compile the information in the general ledger into the basic financial statements: the balance sheet and income statement. How often should this happen? From a manager's point of view, basic financial statements should be prepared in a timely fashion so any unexpected trends in revenues and expenses can be detected and addressed. Most businesses find monthly statements adequate, although firms operating under very stable economic conditions find quarterly or annual financial statements sufficient.

Compiling and preparing financial statements usually necessitates making adjustments to general ledger account balances. Adjustments? Why do we need adjustments? Why can't the accountants get it right the first time? No matter how diligent and efficient the accountants, adjustments will be needed to correct certain account balances. For example, it is customary to analyze accounts receivable to determine if individual outstanding accounts are actually collectable. Any accounts deemed uncollectable are written off, and this requires an adjustment.

Accounts involving fixed assets and depreciation almost always require some adjustment. Most firms record depreciation expense based on the assets on hand at the beginning of the period. These entries are not changed each month to reflect new asset additions or asset retirements.

If a business maintains ending inventory, the balance recorded in the general ledger account must be reconciled with the actual physical count of inventory on hand at the end of the period. Finally, all other accrual accounts involving prepaids and deferrals also need to be analyzed and, perhaps adjusted.

Aggregating account balances on a worksheet called a **trial balance** facilitates the adjustment process. An example of a trial balance follows. The first column of this worksheet is simply a list of all general ledger accounts, starting with the balance sheet accounts and ending with the income statement accounts. The next columns show the account balances before adjustments.

Joint Ventures Trial Balance 12/31/04

Account #	Account	Unadjusted Balance Debit	Credit	Adjustments Debit	Credit	Adjusted Trial Balance Debit	Credit	Balance Sheet Debit	Credit	Income Statement Debit	Credit
101	Cash in Bank	4,162			24	4,138		4,138			
104	Accounts Receivable	15,000				15,000		15,000			
105	Prepaid Expenses	1,275				1,275		1,275			
150	Equipment	14,564				14,564		14,564			
151	Accumulated Depreciation		1,235		2,081		3,316		3,316		
201	Accounts Payable		2,691				2,691		2,691		
210	Fed Tax W/H		360				360		360		
212	State Tax W/H		120				120		120		
213	FICA W/H		112				112		112		
214	Medicare W/H		26				26		26		
215	U.C Taxes Payable		105				105		105		
216	FICA & Medicare Payable		138				138		138		
220	Deferred Revenue		7,500	1,500			6,000		6,000		
230	Notes Payable		6,275		350		6,625		6,625		
301	Owner's Equity		12,500				12,500		12,500		
302	Owner's Draw	19,500				19,500		19,500			
400	Delivery Revenue		145,000		1,500		146,500				146,500
502	Equipment Rent	12,000				12,000				12,000	
503	Office Rent	6,600				6,600				6,600	
504	Depreciation			2,081		2,081				2,081	
505	Office Supplies	408				408				408	
506	Professional Fees	7,380				7,380				7,380	
507	Advertising	2,640				2,640				2,640	
508	Phone	2,016				2,016				2,016	
509	Contract Labor	26,400				26,400				26,400	
520	Wages	43,200				43,200				43,200	
521	FICA Taxes	2,678				2,678				2,678	
522	Medicare Taxes	626				626				626	
523	Unemployment Taxes	336				336				336	
524	Repairs & Maintnance	956				956				956	
525	Airplane Fuel	14,562				14,562				14,562	
526	Automobile	936				936				936	
527	Meals & Entertainment	576				576				576	
528	Dues & Subscriptions	195				195				195	
529	Continuing Education	52				52				52	
530	Interest Expense			350		350				350	
531	Bank Charges			24		24				24	
		176,062	176,062	3,955	3,955	178,493	178,493	54,477	31,993	124,016	146,500
	Net Income(Loss)								22,484	22,484	

Patterns in Adjusting Entries

Adjusting entries follow the same debit/credit form used for recording transactions during the year. The entries themselves are first recorded in a general journal and then posted to the appropriate general ledger account. Unlike other recorded transactions, these adjusting entries are also posted on the trial balance. These entries usually involve standard pairings of balance sheet and income statement accounts. For example, an adjustment to accounts receivable almost always requires an offsetting adjustment to a revenue or sales account. Here is a list of typical account pairings found in adjustment entries:

Adjusting Entry Patterns	
Balance Sheet Account	**Offsetting Income Statement Account**
Accounts Receivable	Revenue or Sales
Prepaid Insurance	Insurance Expense
Inventory	Purchases or Cost of Goods Sold
Prepaid Rent	Rent Expense
Deferred Revenue	Revenue
Accounts Payable	Various Expense Accounts

Adjustments very often go in both directions. The balance sheet accounts may require increases or decreases, so the corresponding income statement accounts also must increase or decrease in offsetting fashion. In making adjusting entries, you might need to debit a revenue account, or credit an expense account, even though you would rarely see this pattern in recording ordinary transactions. In the adjustment process it is not unusual for the same account to require more than one adjustment, with the adjustments made in opposite directions. One adjusting entry can increase a revenue account, and another adjusting entry can decrease the same revenue account.

Example. In analyzing the account balances for *Joint Ventures* at the end of the most recent accounting period, the bookkeeper has discovered that the following accounts need adjustment:

a. Because of fixed asset additions during the year, it was determined that depreciation expense was understated by $2,081.
b. An analysis of the deferred revenue account indicated that the account was overstated by $1,500.

c. A $350 payment of interest on a loan was incorrectly recorded as a principal repayment.

d. In reconciling the checking account, it was determined that $24 of bank service charges had not been recorded.

The journal entries reflecting these adjustments are as follows:

Account #		Dr	Cr
	Joint Ventures		
	Adjusting Entries		
	12/31/2004		
504	Depreciation	2,081	
151	Accumulated Depreciation		2,081
220	Deferred Revenue	1,500	
400	Delivery Revenue		1,500
530	Interest Expense	350	
230	Notes Payable		350
531	Bank Charges	24	
101	Cash in Bank		24
		$3,955	$3,955

Posting Adjusting Entries

After the adjusting entries are posted in the middle columns of the trial balance, the account balances are extended across to the next column, the adjusted balance column. The final columns on the right of the trial balance are used to construct the basic financial statements: the balance sheet and the income statement.

Closing Journal Entries

The final step in the year-end adjustment process is the preparation of closing entries that bring the income statement accounts to zero. Why is this needed? Generally, businesses want to track balances in these accounts for one year at a time. It would not do for current year revenues and expenses to be aggregated with prior year amounts. So, at the beginning of each new accounting period the income and expense balances should be zero. This means that the aggregate balances from the prior period have to be eliminated. How do we eliminate an entire period's balances in these accounts?

Recall that income and expense accounts are sub-categories of the equity section of the balance sheet. A sub-account of the equity category called **Prior Year Income** or **Retained Earnings** is used to transfer all year end income and expense account balances. In the case of sole proprietorships these account balances are closed directly to the **Owner's Equity** account.

Example. Based upon the final adjusted income statement account balances shown in the last columns of the trial balance, *Joint Ventures'* closing entry would be as follows:

		Joint Ventures		
		12/31/2004		
		Closing Entries		
Date	**Acct. #**	**Account**	**Debit**	**Credit**
12/31/2004	400	Delivery revenue	$146,500	
	502	Equipment Rent		$12,000
	503	Office rent		6,600
	504	Depreciation		2,081
	505	Office Supplies		408
	506	Professional Fees		7,380
	507	Advertising		2,640
	508	Phone		2,016
	509	Contract Labor		26,400
	520	Wages		43,200
	521	FICA Taxes		2,678
	522	Medicare Taxes		626
	523	Unemployment Taxes		336
	524	Repairs Maintenance		956
	525	Airplane fuel		14,562
	526	Automobile		936
	527	Meals & Entertainment		576
	528	Dues & Subscriptions		195
	529	Continuing Education		52
	530	Interest Expense		350
	531	Bank Charges		24
	301	Owner's Equity		22,484

Remember: asset, liability and equity accounts are never closed. These balances are carried from period to period.

Financial Statement Preparation

After all adjustments are made the final two columns of the trial balance can be used to prepare the balance sheet and income statement. GAAP also requires the preparation of two other financial statements: the Statement of Cash Flow and the Statement of Owner's Equity.

The Balance Sheet and the Fundamental Accounting Equation

The balance sheet follows the fundamental accounting equation: Assets = Liabilities + Equity. *Joint Ventures'* Balance Sheet is shown here. The balances shown are the amounts in the accounts at the end of the period reported.

Joint Ventures
Balance Sheet
as of December 31, 2004

Assets

Current Assets		
Cash in Bank	$	4,138
Accounts Receivable		15,000
Prepaid Expenses		1,275
Total Current Assets		20,413
Non Current Assets		
Equipment		14,564
Accumulated Depreciation		(3,316)
Total Non Current Assets		11,248
Total Assets	$	31,661

Liabilities and Equity

Liabilities		
Current Liabilities		
Accounts Payable	$	2,691
Fed Tax W/H		360
State Tax W/H		120
FICA W/H		112
Medicare W/H		26
U.C Taxes Payable		105
FICA & Medicare Payable		138
Deferred Revenue		6,000
Total Current Liabilities		9,552
Non Current Liabilities		
Notes Payable		6,625
Total Liabilities		16,177
Equity		
Owner's Equity		12,500
Current Year Income (Loss)		22,484
Less: Owner's Draws		(19,500)
Total Owner's Equity		15,484
Total Liabilities and Equity	$	31,661

Accountants are very particular about the format of financial statements. GAAP prefers a **classified format**, which classifies assets and liabilities as **current** or **non-current**. An asset is deemed current if it is likely to be converted to cash within one year. This usually includes accounts receivable and inventory.

Assets not considered current are deemed non-current. Current assets are generally listed in order of **liquidity**. Liquidity just means the ability to be converted to cash. Liabilities are also classified as current and non-current. **Current liabilities** are those which are expected to be paid off within a year. All other liabilities are classified as non-current.

The Income Statement

The income statement shows the revenue and expense account balances at the end of an accounting period. They reflect income and expenses over the entire accounting period. *Joint Ventures'* income statement follows. If revenue exceeds expenses a business has net income or profit, if expenses exceed revenue the business shows a loss.

Joint Ventures
Income Statement
for the Year Ended December 31,2004

Income	$	%
Delivery Revenue	$ 146,500	100.00%
Expenses		
Equipment Rent	12,000	8.20%
Office Rent	6,600	4.50%
Depreciation	2,081	1.40%
Office Supplies	408	0.30%
Professional Fees	7,380	5.00%
Advertising	2,640	1.80%
Phone	2,016	1.40%
Contract Labor	26,400	18.00%
Wages	43,200	29.50%
FICA Taxes	2,678	1.80%
Medicare Taxes	626	0.40%
Unemployment Taxes	336	0.20%
Repairs & Maintenance	956	0.70%
Airplane Fuel	14,562	9.90%
Automobile	936	0.60%
Meals & Entertainment	576	0.40%
Dues & Subscriptions	195	0.10%
Continuing Education	52	0.00%
Interest Expense	350	0.20%
Bank Charges	24	0.00%
Total Expenses	124,016	84.70%
Net Income(Loss)	$ 22,484	15.30%

The form of the income statement is usually dictated by the nature of the business. A simple service business income statement usually is divided into two sections, one for income and one for expenses. Retail and wholesale businesses usually show sales, cost of goods sold, and gross profit together, with other expenses separately. Manufacturing companies follow a similar format, but may separate marketing from general and administrative expenses.

The Statement of Cash Flows: Show Me the Money!

Many businesses use accrual accounting to reflect a reasonably complete picture of their economic performance over the accounting period. Nonetheless, at some point all accrual assets and liabilities must be reducible to cash. Assets that could not be converted into cash would have limited value. A firm's ability to convert assets to cash is critical to its long-term survival. Because of the importance of cash flow, GAAP requires that companies prepare a financial statement that shows cash flows for the accounting period. *Joint Ventures'* Statement of Cash Flow follows.

Joint Ventures
Statement of Cash Flows
for the Year Ended December 31,2004

Cash From Operations	
Income from continuing operations	$ 22,484
Adjustments to reconcile income to net cash from operations	
Depreciation	2,081
Accounts Receivable	(15,000)
Accounts Payable	2,691
Deferred Revenue	6,000
Accrued Taxes	861
Net cash from operations	19,117
Cash Flows from Investing	
Capital expenditures	(6,500)
Cash Flows from Financing	
Notes payable	6,625
Owner Draws	(19,500)
Net Cash Flows from Financing	(12,875)
Increase (decrease) in cash	(258)
Cash, beginning of the year	4,396
Cash, end of the year	$ 4,138

The statement divides cash flows into three components: cash flows from operations, cash flows from investing activities and cash flows from financing activities.

Operating activities are the ordinary buying and selling activity of a business. **Investing activities** comprise the purchase and retirement of fixed assets, as well as investment in other businesses. **Financing activities** are cash flows derived from the issuance and repayment of long-term debt, and cash flows from equity contributions and draws to owners.

These cash flow categories are used so the users of financial statements do not draw false conclusions about a business, simply because of the net cash increase or decrease over the accounting period. A business always seeks a positive cash flow, particularly from operating activities. However, short-term negative cash flows from operating activities do not necessarily mean that a business is unhealthy.

In fact, during periods of rapid expansion it is not uncommon for companies to experience negative cash flow, because as credit sales increase, so do accounts receivable. Similarly, economic growth often is accompanied by increases in inventory, which also uses up cash. For these reasons, a user of financial statements must be careful not to jump to conclusions about the meaning of positive or negative cash flows.

The Statement of Owner's Equity

The income statement represents changes in an owner's equity derived from the selling and buying activities of the business. Changes in owner's equity may also reflect cash contributions from, and distributions to, the owners. The Statement of Owner's Equity reflects a summary of all components of the changes in owner's equity during the year. The Statement of Owner's Equity for *Joint Ventures* follows.

Joint Ventures Statement of Owner's Equity for the Year Ended December 31,2004	
Balance January 1, 2004	$ 12,500
Net Income	22,484
Cash Withdrawals	(19,500)
Balance December 31, 2004	$ 15,484

Summary

- Account balances must be periodically compiled into financial statements: the balance sheet, the income statement, the cash flow statement and the statement of changes in equity.
- Because accrual accounting requires the use of estimates it is important that these estimates be evaluated and if need be corrected before the financial statements are compiled. These adjustments are called adjusting journal entries.
- Income and expense account balances must be closed at the end of an accounting year. Making a closing entry transfers the year-end balances. This entry transfers the cumulative balances of all income and expense to an equity account.
- Classified balance sheets distinguish between current and non-current assets and liabilities.
- A Statement of Cash Flows is useful because on a long-term basis a firm must be able to efficiently convert its assets into cash. In analyzing cash flows it is useful to distinguish between cash flow from ordinary business operations and cash flow from investing and financing activities.

Exercises

1. What income statement account is adjusted when accounts receivable is adjusted?
2. What income statement account is adjusted when prepaid insurance is adjusted?
3. What income statement account is adjusted when inventory is adjusted?
4. What income statement account is adjusted when prepaid rent is adjusted?
5. What income statement account is adjusted when deferred revenue is adjusted?
6. What income statement account is adjusted when accounts payable is adjusted?
7. What is a closing entry? Why is a closing entry needed?
8. What is a classified balance sheet?
9. Describe the three types of cash flow analyzed in a statement of Cash Flow.

Problems

1. The *Getalife Health Food Store* unadjusted trial balance as of 12/31/04 is shown below. In the closing process the following items require adjusting journal entries:

    a. $126 of previously unrecorded bank charges needs to be recorded.

    b. Accounts receivable is overstated by $300.

    c. The correct ending inventory balance should be $6,250.

    d. Depreciation expense is understated by $1,500.

Journalize these adjustments and post to a full working trial balance. Extend and complete the trial balance. Prepare a closing entry. Prepare a balance sheet and income statement.

Getalife Health Food Store
Trial Balance
12/31/2004

Account #	Account	Unadjusted Debit	Balance Credit	Adjustments Debit	Adjustments Credit	Balance Sheet Debit	Balance Sheet Credit	Income Statement Debit	Income Statement Credit
101	Cash in Bank	15,300							
104	Accounts Receivable	3,500							
105	Prepaid Expenses	1,400							
110	Inventory	6,450							
150	Equipment	110,000							
151	Accumulated Depreciation		15,000						
201	Accounts Payable		15,600						
210	Fed Tax W/H		850						
212	State Tax W/H		220						
213	FICA W/H		300						
214	Medicare W/H		85						
215	U.C Taxes Payable		70						
216	FICA & Medicare Payable		385						
230	Notes Payable		22,500						
301	Owner's Equity		35,000						
302	Owner's Draw	25,000							
400	Product Sales		340,550						
410	Cost of Goods Sold	125,000							
503	Rent & Utilities	25,175							
504	Depreciation	2,500							
505	Office Supplies	785							
506	Professional Fees	3,250							
507	Advertising	18,500							
508	Phone	2,100							
509	Contract Labor	1,500							
520	Wages	78,000							
521	FICA Taxes	4,836							
522	Medicare Taxes	1,131							
523	Unemployment Taxes	475							
524	Repairs & Maintnance	1,056							
525	Shipping & Postage	2,150							
526	Travel	850							
527	Meals & Entertainment	699							
528	Dues & Subscriptions	680							
529	Continuing Education	175							
530	Interest Expense								
531	Bank Charges	48							
		430,560	430,560						

Chapter 10

**Could there be something rotten
in the statements of Denmark?**

In This Chapter

- The Usefulness of the Balance Sheet
- Measuring Economic Performance
- Comparative Measures of Economic Performance
- Using Historical Financial Statements to Predict
  Future Performance
- The Reliability and Accuracy of Financial Statements

The Usefulness and Reliability of Small Business Financial Statements: Passing the Smell Test

How useful and reliable are small business financial statements? Do small business firms' balance sheets reliably and accurately reflect their economic condition? Do their income statements reliably and accurately reflect their economic performance? Let's consider the balance sheet first.

The Usefulness of the Balance Sheet: The Whole and the Sum of the Parts

One of the most basic questions for any business owner is "What is my business worth?" From a lender's standpoint, the most useful questions are "Does the company maintain sufficient liquidity to repay interest and principle?" and "What is the value of the assets used to collateralize my loan?" Because the balance sheet lists assets, liabilities, and equity, it should be useful in answering these questions.

Going Concern Versus Liquidating Value

The balance sheet, despite sometimes being called the statement of net worth, does not always give a clear picture of the entire worth of a business. In fact, often the balance sheet gives a far better picture of the **liquidating value** of the business, as compared to its **going concern value**. The liquidating value is the amount that would be realized in cash if the assets were sold piece-meal, and the liabilities satisfied from the proceeds. Liquidating value is generally applied to a business that will cease operations.

In contrast, the going concern value of a business is the sale price of all the assets, purchased together, under the assumption that the new owners will continue to operate the business. Often, this going concern value is significantly greater than the liquidating value. The difference between the going concern value and the liquidating values is called **goodwill**. What creates goodwill?

Goodwill reflects a firm's ability to retain customers based on prior performance. Essentially, if a business does a good job providing a product or service, its customers are likely to be repeat customers. The distinction between going concern and liquidating value can be illustrated by the following example.

Example. Carlo Castrato has run a successful ball bearing company for several years. If he decided to sever operations, close his doors, and sell his equipment and furnishings, he might realize $25,000. This is the liquidating value of the assets. On the other hand, his nephew Carmine is willing to pay him $225,000 for the same equipment if he can use the firm's name and operate at the same location. The difference between the liquidating value and the going concern value is $200,000, reflecting the goodwill that Carlo has built over the years.

Why would Carmine be willing to pay $200,000 for equipment and furnishings that he could purchase for $25,000? Because, if he opens up a new ball bearing company at a different location under a different name, it may take several years to reach the level of profitability currently being realized by Castrato. The ability to step into his uncle's shoes allows Carmine to make considerably more profit immediately.

Although this example may seem extreme, it is not. Most businesses that have operated successfully over several years are able to command going concern value. If goodwill is such a common and valuable asset, why doesn't GAAP require that it be reflected on the balance sheet? Simply put, there is no one reliable and universally accepted method to measure the goodwill of a business.

While there are many theories and methods of valuing goodwill, until a business actually goes through the laborious negotiation process involved in selling its entire operation, the actual value of goodwill is not precisely determinable. The appraisal of goodwill is more art than science. For this reason, GAAP allows the recognition of goodwill on the balance sheet only after one business has actually acquired another business.

Absent an actual purchase, GAAP believes that allowing management to determine the value of its own internally generated goodwill would lead to wildly inflated valuations, with little ground in economic reality.

However, because goodwill is not reflected on most small business balance sheets, these statements generally do not provide an accurate assessment of the worth of a firm as a whole.

Creditor Uses of the Balance Sheet

Many businesses find it necessary at some point to borrow funds. Lenders need to assess the credit worthiness of borrowers. Two determinants of credit worthiness are the existence and extent of **collateral** and the **liquidity** of the business. The balance sheet can be useful in assessing both factors. Collateral are those assets that are pledged by a lender to secure a loan. Even though assets, particularly fixed assets, are not carried at current fair market values on the balance sheet, the lender can determine the kind of assets the business owns and the extent of debt to other lenders. It is usually not difficult for lenders to reach reasonable estimates of the current liquidating values of most business assets, so their absence on the balance sheet usually is not a major problem.

Liquidity is another useful determinant of credit worthiness. Liquidity refers to the availability of cash to the business. Obviously, lenders are concerned whether borrowers will have sufficient cash to repay loans. Liquidity is mainly a function of profitability. Ordinarily, the more profitable the business, the more cash available. However, liquidity is not simply a function of profitability, and firms of comparable profitability do not necessarily have comparable liquidity.

Other factors affecting liquidity are the rates at which accounts receivable and inventory are converted to cash. A business that collects its accounts receivable in an average of 20 days generally has more cash on hand than a business that requires 45 days. Similarly, a business that turns over its inventory 15 times a year has more cash on hand than a company that turns its inventory only 10 times a year.

Another indication of relative liquidity is the ratio of current assets to current liabilities. All other things being equal, a business that has a higher ratio of current assets to current liabilities is more liquid than a company with a lower ratio. A company's balance sheet may be used by a creditor to measure its liquidity through the use of **ratio analysis**.

Some Common Liquidity Ratios

The two most widely used liquidity ratios are the **current ratio** and the **quick ratio**.

$$\text{Current Ratio} = \frac{\text{Current Assets}}{\text{Current Liabilities}}$$

Looking back at *Joint Ventures'* balance sheet, notice that it had $20,413 of current assets and $9,552 of current liabilities. This yields a current ratio of 2.13:

$$\frac{20,413}{9,552} = 2.13$$

Because certain current assets, such as inventory and prepaids, are not immediately convertible to cash, the quick ratio is often used as an alternative measure of liquidity.

$$\text{Quick Ratio} = \frac{\text{Quick Assets}}{\text{Current Liabilities}}$$

Quick assets are cash, marketable securities and receivables. *Joint Ventures'* quick assets are $19,138, yielding a quick ratio of 2.00:

$$\frac{19,138}{9,552} = 2.00$$

Generally, creditors want these ratios to at least equal to one. If the ratios fall below one, the firm's current liabilities exceed its current or quick assets, which is not good if you are a creditor.

Another important set of liquidity ratios for a business with significant credit sales is the **Accounts Receivable Turnover** and **Average Collection Period** ratios.

$$\text{Accounts Receivable Turnover} = \frac{\text{Credit Sales}}{\text{Average Accounts Receivable}}$$

Credit sales are all non-cash sales. Average accounts receivable is the average of the beginning and end of period balances. The higher the turnover, the better the collections experience.

Assuming that all $90,000 of *Joint Ventures'* delivery revenue was credit sales, and its average net accounts receivable was $15,000, the accounts receivable turnover would be six:

$$\frac{90,000}{15,000} = 6$$

An even more useful measure of the effectiveness of a businesses collections is the Average Collection Period:

$$\text{Average Collection Period} = \frac{365}{\text{Accounts Receivable Turnover}}$$

This is a more useful ratio because it computes the average number of days it takes to collect accounts receivable. If a business extends credit for 30 days, its average collection period should not be much greater than 30.

Since *Joint Ventures'* accounts receivable turnover was six, its average collection period would be about 60 days:

$$\frac{365}{6} = 60.8 \text{ days}$$

This collection period would be considered too long if the firm's policy is to demand payment in 30 days.

For businesses that sell inventory a very important liquidity measure is *Inventory Turnover.*

$$\text{Inventory Turnover} = \frac{\text{Cost of Goods Sold}}{\text{Average Inventory}}$$

Average inventory is the average of the beginning and ending inventory. What does inventory turnover measure? It literally measures how quickly inventory sells. The higher the ratio, the more quickly the inventory moves. Quick turnover is desirable because it means that goods are more quickly turned into cash. A quick turnover of inventory may be an indication that a firm is selling the right products. On the other hand, too quick a turnover may mean that a company is pricing its products too low.

Example. Janis had $50,000 of cost of goods sold and an average inventory of $2,500 during the recent year. This means that her inventory turnover was 20 (50,000/2,500). This may seem like a reasonable turnover for her product. But is it? It would help to have information about other firms' operating in the same industry. For most types of firms such information is available. Some widely used databases for developing such benchmarks are described in Appendix 2.

Leverage Ratios

Creditors also are interested in a debtor firm's **leverage**. Leverage is the to degree which a business finances itself with debt, instead of equity. Increasing reliance on debt increases the rate of return on equity in a profitable business, but also increases the risk of going under, due to too much debt. Here is an example of how leverage works.

Example. Hansel and Gretel Grimm are contemplating opening a guided tour company called *Babes in the Woods*. They project they will need to raise $10,000 to start operations. They have a choice of borrowing half the needed funds, or using only their own funds. They believe the business will generate about $1,000 a year in net profit. If they do no borrowing their equity will be $10,000, and the expected **return on equity** (net income/equity) will be 10% ($1,000/$10,000). On the other hand if they borrow $5,000 and use just $5,000 of their own funds, the expected return will be 20%($1,000/$5,000).

Although leverage is often regarded favorably by borrowers, creditors view it negatively. A high degree of investment by owners provides a greater incentive for the owners to succeed. If the owners have very little of their own money invested, it is psychologically easier for the owners to walk away from a struggling business. Creditors, thus, want to lend to firms in which the owners have a large investment. A common measure of leverage is the **debt to equity ratio**.

Debt to Equity Ratio = $\dfrac{\text{Total Debt}}{\text{Total Owner's Equity}}$

In small to medium sized business, it is not uncommon to have ratios of between 3 and 4. This means for every dollar the owner contributes, there is between $3 and $4 of debt. *Joint Ventures'* total debt was $16,177 and its total equity was $15,484, yielding a debt to equity ratio of a little over 1.

$$\frac{16,177}{15,484} = 1.04$$

Measuring Small Firms' Economic Performance: The Profit versus Compensation Problem

The goal of the income statement is to reflect how well a business performed in the most recent accounting period. A business performs well to the extent it earns net income or profit. Unfortunately, small business income statements often do not accurately reflect profit. In many cases, financial statements misrepresent profit as compensation expense. In other cases the statements misreport compensation expense as profit. As we will see, distinguishing between profit and compensation expense can be problematic.

Economic Profit versus Compensation

In many, if not most, small firms the owners are actively engaged in operating the business. These owners contribute investment dollars **and** many hours of full time service to their businesses. Cash payments from a firm to its owners can be considered as either returns on owner investment or compensation for services provided. Unfortunately, GAAP provides no reliable means to distinguish between returns on investment versus compensation for owner labor. Only the former constitutes economic profits. The latter constitutes wages.

The Classification of Payments to Owners Based on the Form of Ownership

Under GAAP, payments made to owners of unincorporated firms are never classified as wages. Such payments are always recorded as owner or partner draws in the equity section of the balance sheet. This is the case, even if the cash withdrawals are in substance payments for services the owner renders to the business. Such payments should be considered wages, because if the owner did not provide the services the business would have to pay an employee wages to do so. An example will clarify this point.

Example. Consider two law firms. *Steve Stickum Law Office* operates as a sole proprietorship and, hence, is unincorporated. *Charles Churnum SC* operates as a corporation. Both firms have $300,000 of revenue and $175,000 of expenses not related to payments for owner labor. In each firm, the owner is an attorney who works 3,000 hours per year and is responsible for virtually all revenue generated. Cash withdrawals paid to Steve Stickum are classified as owner withdrawals that reduce equity and are **not** reflected in the income statement. Cash payments made to Charles Churnum are classified as wages and are reflected on the income statement. Here is a side by side comparison of the two income statements:

A Tale of Two Law Firms		
	Stickum Law Office	**Churnum SC**
Revenue	$ 300,000	$ 300,000
Non-Owner Expenses	175,000	175,000
Owner Compensation	-	125,000
Total Expenses	175,000	300,000
Net Income	$ 125,000	$ -

It appears that Stickum is significantly more profitable than Churnum SC, but from an economic point of view both firms perform identically. For Steve's firm, form is trumping substance. GAAP does not require firms to reflect payments for owner labor as expense, because management would have to decide how much of the cash withdrawals reflect a wage payment and how much reflects a return on investment.

Such allocations often are subjective and difficult to make.

Another problem is that there often is not enough cash generated by a business to adequately compensate an owner for his or her services. Consider this example.

Example. Two retail companies in the same product line have $500,000 of sales, $250,000 cost of goods sold, and $250,000 of non-owner expenses. The owner of the *Eke Company* contributes no significant services to the business. On the other hand, the owner of the *Squeak Company* works 3,500 hours a year in the business. Since neither company had sufficient cash to pay the owners, neither owner received any cash. This is what the income statements look like side by side.

A Tale of Two Retailers		
	Eke	**Squeak**
Sales	$ 500,000	$ 500,000
Cost of Sales	250,000	250,000
Gross Profit	250,000	250,000
Non-Owner Expense	250,000	250,000
Net Income	$ -	$ -

It appears from the income statements that both companies had the same lackluster, break-even performance. But the economic performance of *Squeak* was much worse than *Eke's*, because *Squeak* required significant services from its owner, simply to break even. *Eke* broke even without such services. Even if GAAP required firms to distinguish payments to owners as either wages or profit, economic distortions like these would continue to exist.

Income Tax Incentives in the Classification of Payments as Wages versus Profit

The decision to classify cash payments to owners as wages versus profit is often affected by tax considerations. The tax code recognizes two forms of corporation, a C Corporation and an S corporation. When a corporation of either type makes payments to owners that are not classified as wages, the payments are called dividends. Dividend payments to owners are considered distributions of corporate profits. With the C Corporation, dividend payments are taxed twice, once at the corporate level and once again at the individual level. With the S Corporation, dividend payments to owners are not taxed at the corporate level, but are taxed only on the individual owner's tax return.

Firms operating as C corporations have an incentive to classify payments to owners as wages to avoid double taxation. With the S Corporation, there is no need to classify dividend payments as wages to avoid double taxation. In fact, there is an incentive to avoid classifying such payments as wages, even though they are. S Corporation dividends are not subject to employment taxes, such as Social Security and Medicare taxes; wage payments are.

Example. Jeff Skewing owns and manages a small natural gas trading corporation called *Endrun, Inc.*, which is classified as a C corporation. Assume that after all other expenses, the corporation has $100,000 available to pay Skewing. The corporation's comptroller, Andy Fastalk, indicates that a case could be made for classifying some of the payments as wages and some as dividends. If they want to be aggressive, they might get away with classifying all as one or the other. According to Fastalk, the tax savings dictate it would be best to classify all payments as wages and none as dividends. Fastalk works up the following comparisons, which assumes a corporate tax rate of 30%, an individual tax rate of 25%, and a payroll tax rate of 15%. The payroll tax is split between the employee owner and the corporation.

Endrun C Corporation Tax Comparison		
	Payments as Dividends	**Payments as Wages**
Corporate Income Tax	$ 30,000	$ -
Corporate Payroll Tax	-	7,500
Individual Income Tax	25,000	25,000
Individual Payroll Tax	-	7,500
Total Taxes	55,000	40,000
Savings from classifying payments as wages		$ 15,000

Assume the same facts, except that *Endrun* is an S rather than a C corporation. As you can see the net tax advantages are exactly the *opposite* from a C corporation. In the former case, tax incentives motivate a classification of payments as wages. In an S corporation classification of payments as dividends yields tax savings.

Endrun S Corporation Tax Comparison		
	Payments as Dividends	Payments as Wages
Corporate Income Tax	$ -	$ -
Corporate Payroll Tax	-	7,500
Individual Income Tax	25,000	25,000
Individual Payroll Tax	-	7,500
Total Taxes	25,000	40,000
Savings from classifying payments as dividends		$ 15,000

As you might expect there are IRS rules to prevent corporations from manipulating facts and circumstances to achieve lower taxes. In the case of C corporations, the rules are designed to prevent corporations from classifying payments as wages if they should be classified as dividends. In the case of S corporations, the rules are designed to prevent corporations from classifying payments as dividends if they should be classified as wages. However, these rules are usually effective only in the extreme cases. For example, someone claiming $200,000 of wages for doing only a few hours of work would be a clear case. Similarly, someone claiming $200,000 as dividends and nothing as wages even though they worked 3,000 hours per year, would also be a clear case. In the very common, less extreme cases, distinguishing wages from dividends is more difficult.

Intangible Returns to Owners

Direct cash payments to owners are not the only source of problems in assessing the profitability of small businesses. Frequently, small business owners pay themselves lavish fringe benefits in the form of travel, automobile, entertainment, and meal expenses. These payments may greatly exceed the amounts that would be paid to non-owner employees. In this way, profits may be understated.

Another important aspect of small business performance that is not adequately reflected in the income statements concerns the quality of the owner's life. In most small firms the owner spends many hours working in the business. This work experience may be largely positive or largely negative. However, the overall level of satisfaction the owner derives from owning and operating the business may not be directly related to the cash compensation received. In many cases, the relationship may be inverse. Consider this example.

Example. Greg Grind, CPA, has a client Larry Laidback, a professional folk guitarist. Every year at tax time, Greg reviews Larry's income statement. Very rarely has Larry's net income exceeded $20,000 per year. One year Greg asked Larry how many hours he works per year. Larry estimated that promotional activities, rehearsals, song writing and performances account for about 60 hour a week, or about 3,000 hours per year. Greg quickly calculated that Larry makes about $6.70 per hour. Greg smugly thought to himself that he nets about $120,000 per year working only about 2,000 hours. This translates to $60 per hour, approaching ten times the hourly compensation of Larry. Greg asked Larry if he ever thought about how much he makes per hour. Larry laughed and said "No, because I have enough to live on and I am doing exactly what I want to be doing in life." As Larry's answer sunk in, Greg's smugness turned to sadness because he could never say that his work represented exactly what he wanted to do with his life.

In this example Larry's business offers him personal satisfactions that are not reflected on his income statement. Greg's business related dissatisfactions are not reflected on his income statement. For small business owners, the satisfactions or dissatisfactions derived from operating their firms constitutes important positive or negative returns that income statements are incapable of quantifying.

Comparative Measures of Economic Performance

As we have just seen, it can be very difficult to measure a firm's economic performance in any *absolute* sense. Financial statements are in general much better at reflecting relative measures of economic performance. Relative measures include comparisons between this year's economic performance and prior years, or this year's performance compared with expected or budgeted performance. If reliable comparative data is available, it is sometimes possible to compare one company's performance against the performance of other businesses in the same field.

Converting Raw Numbers to Relative Numbers

Comparing the raw numbers on financial statements over several accounting periods can yield misleading interpretations of economic performance for several reasons. First, over several periods of time the value of the dollars reported on financial statements change, due to inflation or deflation. To a certain extent, this problem can be overcome by adjusting the raw numbers using a **price index**, which attempts to equalize the purchasing power of dollars over different accounting periods. These indices are far from perfect, but they do help when comparing the raw numbers on multi-year financial statements. However, smaller firms may find use of these indices cumbersome.

Another problem in comparing raw numbers on financial statements is that over many accounting periods the nature and size of a firm's activity can change dramatically. In the start-up period, the volume of sales is not likely to be as great as the volumes achieved as a business matures. Also, the mix of products and services offered by a business may change dramatically over time.

To compensate for changes in the value of the dollar and changes in the scope and nature of business activities, financial statements are often converted to percentages. In converting raw numbers on an income statement to percentages, the total revenue or sales figure is usually used as the basis for percentage conversion. If a business has $100,000 in total revenue, this is converted to 100%. All expenses are converted to percentages by dividing the raw expense numbers into the raw total revenue number. For example if the firm incurs $30,000 of salary expenses, salary expenses would be shown at 30% (30,000/100,000). If the raw number for advertising was $4,500 then the percentage for this expense is 4.5% (4,500/100,000). The *Joint Ventures'* Income Statement in Chapter 9 illustrates the conversion of raw numbers to percentages.

How does the conversion of raw numbers to percentages improve the usefulness of multi-period statements? Despite changes in the value of the dollar or the scope of a firm's operations, the relationships between categories of revenue and expenses often remain relatively consistent. Wide variations in percentages from period to period indicate that significant changes in the structure and nature of the operations have taken place.

The stability of the relationship between income and expense items explains how historical operating results can be used to construct operating budgets for future periods. For example, a company may expect its sales to decrease or increase significantly. If certain expenses have shown a stable percentage relationship to total revenue in the past, specific dollar amounts for these expenses can be budgeted, based on the expected dollar amount of revenue.

Using Historical Financial Statements to Predict Future Performance

The income statement tries to indicate how well a business performed in the most recent accounting period. Assuming that such performance is accurately portrayed, can this information help predict the firm's future performance? The answer depends largely on the firm's economic environment.

The Stability of Economic Environments

Some businesses operate in very stable, predictable economic climates; others do not. Economic stability is primarily a function of the demand for a firm's goods and services, the degree of competition, and the cost stability of required goods and services.

Certain goods and services are more essential than others are. For example, because people need food, shelter, and medicine, there will always be a fixed demand for these goods and services. Other goods and services are not as essential. Cosmetics, sports equipment, and leisure travel are examples of less essential goods and services. The overall demand for essential goods and services generally is more stable than the demand for less essential services. Demand for essential services is less likely to fluctuate with upturns and downturns in the economy than demand for less essential services.

In general, a business that supplies essential goods and services will have a more predictable revenue stream than a business that supplies less essential goods and services. Thus, the revenue or sales component of the income statement of a business providing essential goods and services is more useful in predicting future revenue or sales than the income statement of a business providing less essential goods and services.

The degree of competition a business faces is another key factor in the predictability of a firm's earnings. As a rule, the more competitors there are in a particular market, the less control each competitor has over the selling price of its products or services. The less control a firm has over the prices it charges, the less predictable are its revenue and sales.

Finally, the stability of factors of production varies from business to business. A business that sells coffee or high quality chocolate can be adversely affected by rising prices of coffee and cocoa beans. Generally, the supply and cost of labor is more stable than the cost of many raw materials. Thus, the expenses of a service business tend to be more predictable than a business that sells or processes products.

Risk in the Small Business Environment

The most recent performance of a small business, as reflected in its income statement, may give little insight into its future performance, simply because there is a great deal of risk in running **any** small firm. Even the most stable small firms are vulnerable to unexpected disruptions. Because small businesses often rely on the services of the owner or a few key employees, these firms can be adversely affected or absolutely ruined if these contributions are lost or reduced. Death, disability, retirement, divorce, drug addiction, or burnout can turn a profitable business into a losing one in a very short period of time.

Any number of external events can rapidly reverse the fortunes of previously successful small retail businesses. A plant or military base closing can quickly turn a prosperous community into a struggling one. A highway relocation or reconstruction can adversely affect traffic flow and lead to dramatic declines in revenue. The appearance of a Wal-Mart, Home Depot, or Borders can spell doom to previously successful small businesses.

Looking Beyond the Numbers

An income statement may tell you *if* a business did well or badly in the most recent period, but it does not reveal **why** a business performed as it did. Success or failure in business generally results from a combination of many factors, but the two key variables are management skill and luck.

Management skill is needed to insure that the right products and services are sold at the right price. Such skill is also needed to insure that customers and clients are satisfied with the products and services sold. Products and services also need to be marketed effectively. Costs must be controlled, employee morale maintained.

While management skill is an important determinant of success or failure, good and bad luck almost always play an important role in all human affairs. Good luck can allow a less than efficient business to make a profit despite its management failings. On the other hand, with bad luck a company with great management can still suffer losses. Factoring the contributions of management competence and luck in determining the firm's reported operating results in one period is a difficult proposition. On the other hand, the ability to make profits year in and year out indicates that luck is not the only factor at work.

The Reliability and Accuracy of Financial Statements

Financial statements cannot be useful if they are based on unreliable and inaccurate recordings of transactions. There is no greater example of the "garbage in, garbage out" principle than financial statement preparation. The problem is that financial statement users cannot usually assess the presence of garbage simply by reading the statements. The statements may look fine, but in reality be riddled with inaccuracies.

The two main sources of financial statement inaccuracy are deliberate dishonesty and incompetence. There are two principle ways to combat these problems. The first method is to regularly hire an outside accounting firm to **audit** the financial statements. In an audit, the outside accountant tests reported account balances for accuracy. As importantly, the auditor tests to see that the accounting principles used in recording transactions are in conformity with GAAP and applied on a consistent basis. Despite some notorious recent audit failures involving large corporations, the auditing process, in most cases, provides a reasonable safeguard against fraudulent and inaccurate financial reporting.

The second method used to prevent fraudulent and inaccurate financial reporting is the adoption of adequate *internal controls*. Internal controls are the policies and procedures that a business can adopt to safeguard its assets, insure accuracy of financial reporting, and prevent fraud. These methods are not mutually exclusive. In the best of all worlds, firms would have both good internal controls and regular audits.

Unfortunately, hiring outside auditors and having the very best internal controls can be expensive, especially for small firms. The question of how much money should be spent on auditing and internal controls is a matter of perspective and circumstances. For example, a small business owner who uses the financial statements for internal management purposes only, has little incentive to hire an outside auditor. On the other hand small business lenders and outside investors have a much greater need for audited financial statements.

For many, if not most, small businesses, regular audits are an unnecessary expense. The same cannot be said about adequate internal controls. Even the smallest business can benefit from well-designed controls designed to prevent fraud, theft, and accounting errors. In fact, small business owners are more likely to be the victims, rather than the perpetrators, of financial statement fraud. All too frequently a lower level bookkeeper or accountant will "cook the books" in order to cover theft and embezzlement. For this reason, it is important to have some understanding of internal controls.

The Internal Controls in the Small Business Environment

As indicated above, internal controls are the policies and procedures that a firm adopts to safeguard its assets, insure the accuracy of financial reporting, and prevent fraud. Insuring the accuracy of accounting information can involve something as simple as designing transaction registers and journals that minimize the mis-recording of transactions. Other common sense policies involve purchasing reliable accounting software and hiring well-qualified bookkeeping personnel to handle basic accounting tasks.

There are several widely used internal control procedures to prevent employee theft. Three of the most important controls are *employee bonding, segregation and rotation of duties*, and *budgeting*. Bonding is a form of commercial insurance that indemnifies a firm against employee theft. Usually, a background check is required to obtain bonding for any particular employee. Many umbrella commercial insurance policies include blanket employee theft coverage that does not require specific background checks.

Segregation of duties ensures that employees who handle cash or other assets do not also have access to accounting records. This prevents employees with access to both assets and accounting records from covering up their thefts.

Example. Miss Feasance is the bookkeeper for a small law firm. Her job responsibilities include writing out checks and recording the disbursements in the check register and computerized check journal. She is also responsible for performing the monthly bank reconciliation. She notes that the owner never looks at the cancelled checks, so every month she writes a couple of $100 checks to herself, but records the disbursements as payments to a process server the firm uses to serve subpoenas. Neither the owner nor the outside accountant ever look at the cancelled checks. All they see are the entries in the general ledger. Because the firm normally spends between $1,500 and $2,000 per month in legitimate process service costs, the extra $100 or $200 payments go unnoticed.

The above fraud could have been prevented by not letting Miss Feasance have check signing authority. If she had check signing authority, someone else should have entered the disbursements in the general ledger and performed the bank reconciliations.

Another control involves shifting personnel into different job functions on a periodic basis or forcing employees to take vacations and having someone else perform their job functions for a certain period of time. The logic of this internal control is that certain frauds, such as *lapping schemes*, require the fraudster to maintain continuous control over a certain accounting function. Here is an example involving a lapping scheme.

Example. Miss Feasance's bother Mal is the billing clerk for a psychotherapy clinic. He has devised a lapping scheme that works like this: at the beginning of every month he takes two or three payments made to the clinic and deposits the funds in his bank account. To cover this fraud, he does not steal subsequent payments from other customers but instead of crediting the payments to the correct patient accounts, he credits the payments to the patients whose payments he previously stole. In this way the stolen payments are not detected as long as the patients see their accounts credited for the amount they paid. The scheme works as long as there is a steady stream of payments made to the clinic and the lag between payment and crediting is not too great.

Mal Feasance's scheme works as long as he can keep covering previous thefts with subsequent payments. The scheme would be detected if he took a long vacation or had his job responsibilities occasionally performed by some one else.

Budgeting is the process of predicting the operating revenues and expenses for the next accounting period. This process serves as an internal control when owners regularly compare current actual revenue and expense with budgeted amounts. Failure of actual results to fall within a reasonable range of budgeted amounts should cause the owners to investigate the reason for the variance.

Example If the owner of Miss Feasance's law practice would establish budgets for expenses and revenue, the extra $200 per month she was pocketing and recording as process serving fees, might cause a variance that could be investigated.

Failures to Implement Internal Controls

Most frauds occur in small firms because their financial statements are rarely audited and they often lack the resources to implement proper internal controls. For example, many small firms cannot afford the cost of hiring enough staff to implement proper segregation of duties. Another more subtle reason why internal controls are not effectively implemented stems from human psychology.

The premise of internal controls is that people are susceptible to dishonesty and that special efforts must be implemented to protect a firm from its own employees. This is an easy premise to accept when thinking about human beings in the abstract. However, it is more difficult to think of your employees as potentially dishonest. When you work closely with another person over any period of time, it is natural for trust to develop. The conscientious implementation of internal controls in a small business may send a subtle message that there is a lack of this natural trust.

On the other hand, it is precisely this natural willingness to trust that gets many small business owners into trouble. They do not make the psychic effort to implement the needed controls, because the burden of distrusting their own employees is too great. In fact, the shock and anguish of employers who have been betrayed by trusted employees who have acted dishonestly, is often more painful than the monetary loss (which is often insured).

Summary

- Balance sheets often do not reflect the going concern value of a business. Going concern value reflects the amount a buyer would pay for all the firm's assets on the assumption that operations would continue.
- Creditors are concerned with borrowers' ability to repay loans. Liquidity, which is a measure of the availability of cash to a firm, is a useful indicator of credit worthiness. Liquidity can be measured by looking at various ratios of assets and liabilities found on the balance sheet. The balance sheet also allows creditors to assess a firm's leverage, which indicates the degree to which the business is financed with debt.
- Determining the profitability of small businesses from their income statements is very difficult because there is often no clear cut way to determine if payments made to owners are really profits or wages. The form of ownership often dictates classification of these payments on the income statement. Tax considerations often enter into the classification as well. Non cash benefits (and detriments) to the owner of operating the business are not reflected on the income statement.

- Converting income statement numbers to percentages, usually based on total revenue or sales facilitates comparing one year's operating results with past results.
- Care must be taken in predicting future firm performance from its historical operating results. Predictability is a function of the stability of a firm's economic environment. Small businesses face many risks that can rapidly change a successful company into a failing one.
- Income statements may indicate if a business has done well or badly, but they cannot tell you why. Management skill and luck are the greatest determinants of success and failure. To understand the firm's past operating results and future prospects you have to look beyond the numbers.
- Financial statements cannot be useful unless they are accurate and reliable. Reliability and accuracy can be insured to a degree by having the statements audited by an independent accounting firm.
- Reliability and accuracy are also enhanced by the adoption of internal controls. Internal controls are all the measures that a firm adopts to safeguard its assets, insure accuracy of its financial reports and prevent fraud. Employee bonding, segregation of duties and establishment of operating budgets are important internal controls.

Exercises

1. What is the difference between liquidating and going concern value?
2. What creates goodwill?
3. Why does GAAP not record a value for goodwill?
4. What are a creditor's basic concerns about a businesses financial condition?
5. What balance sheet ratios can a creditor use to evaluate a firm's liquidity?
6. Is a high inventory turnover always a good thing?
7. What is leverage?
8. Why is it difficult to measure the profitability of a small business in which the owner provides many hours of labor?
9. Why is it useful to convert raw income statement numbers into percentages when making inter-period comparisons of profitability?
10. What factors affect the stability of a firm's earnings over several years?
11. What factors make predicting a small firm's future earnings difficult?

Problem

1. John White operates a business that produces crackers called *The White Cracker Company*. The financial statements for the current and previous period are shown below. Based upon these financial statements compute the following ratios;

    a. Current ratio.
    b. Quick Ratio
    c. Accounts Receivable Turnover
    d. Average Collection Period
    e. Inventory Turnover
    f. Gross Profit Percentage

Assume all sales are credit sales, i.e., all sales generate receivables.

White Cracker Company
Balance Sheet

Assets	Beginning	Ending
Current Assets		
Cash in Bank	$17,500	$19,800
Inventory	14,000	18,000
Accounts Receivable	36,200	45,000
Prepaid Expenses	2,500	3,600
Total Current Assets	70,200	86,400
Non Current Assets		
Equipment	125,000	135,000
Accumulated Depreciation	(25,000)	(35,000)
Total Non Current Assets	100,000	100,000
Total Assets	$170,200	$186,400
Liabilities and Equity		
Liabilities		
Current Liabilities		
Accounts Payable	$15,200	$17,000
Fed Tax W/H	2,500	2,800
State Tax W/H	1,500	1,800
FICA W/H	2,600	2,700
Medicare W/H	604	631
U.C Taxes Payable	514	520
FICA & Medicare Payable	3,204	3,331
Deferred Revenue	2,500	3,500
Total Current Liabilities	28,622	32,282
Non Current Liabilities		
Notes Payable	75,000	65,000
Total Liabilities	103,622	97,282
Equity		
Owner's Equity	45,000	66,578
Current Year Income (Loss)	56,578	62,540
Less: Owner's Draws	(35,000)	(40,000)
Total Owner's Equity	66,578	89,118
Total Liabilities and Equity	$170,200	$186,400

White Cracker Company
Income Statement

	Prior Year	Current Year
Sales	$ 650,000	$720,000
Cost of Goods Sold	365,000	398,000
Gross Profit	285,000	322,000
Marketing	95,000	105,000
General & Administrative	128,172	149,910
Interest Expense	5,250	4,550
Total Expenses	228,422	259,460
Net Income	$ 56,578	$ 62,540

Appendix 1: Wage Withholdings: A Special Case of Accounts Payable

When a business hires employees the federal government requires that the employer withhold a portion of the employees gross wages to cover income and Social Security taxes. Social Security taxes actually consist of two separate taxes FICA and Medicare. The Medicare tax rate is 1.45% of all gross wages while the FICA rate is 6.2% of gross wages up to a ceiling which changes every year (In 2005 the ceiling was $90,000.). Additionally the employer must pay a dollar for dollar match for every dollar of Medicare and FICA taxes withheld. This means that the government collects 2.9% of total gross wages in Medicare taxes and 12.4% of gross wages up to the annually set ceiling in Social Security taxes.

Furthermore an employer is expected to withhold from an employee's gross wages an amount to cover the expected amount of federal income taxes the employee will owe for the year. Generally the amount withheld will depend upon the amount and frequency of gross wage payments as well as the employee's filing status and number of personal exemptions claimed on his or her income tax return.

In addition to these federal income and Social Security taxes, state and local jurisdictions usually levy some form of income tax and require that employers withhold an amount from each gross pay check to defray these expected liabilities. The amount of required withholdings for these taxes also varies with the frequency and amount of gross pay.

Finally, the federal government and almost all state jurisdictions require that the employer pay into a reserve fund for unemployment insurance. This amount is generally not withheld from employees' gross wages but rather is levied on the employer based on rates determined by the state jurisdiction and the balance in the employer's reserve account.

There is a distinction between taxes that are withheld from employees' wages and taxes that the employer has to pay above the amount of gross wages. The employer's match of Social Security taxes and the unemployment taxes payable to the unemployment reserve account are called employment taxes and they constitute an expense above and beyond gross payroll payments. From an accrual accounting point of view the liabilities for both withholding and payroll taxes should be recorded when payroll checks are issued.

Example. *Joint Ventures* hires a pilot to fly some deliveries and that the pilot, L. Reed, is owed a gross wage of $1,000. Assume the following payroll tax withholdings and payroll tax liabilities associated with this gross payroll:

Gross Wages	1,000
Fed Tax W/H	(150)
State Tax W/H	(50)
FICA W/H	(62)
Medicare W/H	(15)
Net Payroll	723
Employers FICA	62
Employers Medicare	15
Unemployment Taxes	36

The entry when the payroll check is actually issued is as follows:

Date	Acct.#	Account Description	Debit	Credit
1/15/2005	520	Gross Wages	$1,000	
	210	Fed Tax W/H		$ 150
	212	State Tax W/H		50
	213	FICA W/H		62
	214	Medicare W/H		15
	101	Cash in Bank		723
	521	FICA Taxes	62	
	522	Medicare Taxes	15	
	523	Unemployment Taxes	36	
	215	Payroll Taxes Payable		113

Notice that there is no expense associated with payroll taxes withheld. The full expense is reflected in gross wages. Notice also that there are two entries needed at the time the payroll check is issued. One to reflect the gross payroll and withholdings and another to record the employer payroll tax liability.

The payment of withheld taxes represents a very special type of liability for employers. If an employee's gross wages have been subject to tax withholdings then the government credits the employee with taxes paid **whether or not the employer actually turns the withheld taxes over to the government**. Because the government must credit the taxes withheld to the employee, when an employer fails to turn over withheld taxes the government in effect is making an unauthorized loan to the employer. The government does not like making unauthorized loans.

For all the above reasons the penalties for failure to pay over withheld or other payroll taxes are subject to very steep penalties. Furthermore unpaid withheld payroll taxes cannot be discharged in bankruptcy unlike other debts and regular income tax liabilities.

The required timing for paying withheld taxes and other payroll taxes is based upon how much is owed. The greater the amount owed the shorter the period the employer has to make the required payments. The entry for payment of the payroll withholding and taxes is as follows:

Date	Acct.#	Account Description	Debit	Credit
1/15/2005	210	Fed Tax W/H	$ 150	
	212	State Tax W/H	50	
	213	FICA W/H	62	
	214	Medicare W/H	15	
	101	Cash		$ 277
	215	Payroll Taxes Payable	113	
	101	Cash		$ 113

Appendix 2: Sources of Information on Small Closely Held Businesses

As pointed out in the last chapter it is usually very helpful to compare a particular company's operating performance and financial condition with the performance and condition of other similar companies. The key tool for such comparisons is ratio analysis.

There are six widely used sources of information on small closely held businesses:

1. Almanac of Business and Industrial Financial Ratios
2. RMA Annual Statement Studies
3. Financial Studies of Small Business
4. IRS Corporate Ratios
5. IRS Corporate Financial Ratios
6. Financial Ratio Analyst

Sources of Data

With the exception of RMA and the Financial Studies of Small Business all other sources derive data from corporate tax returns filed with the IRS. These tax returns represent a sample from all corporate income tax returns filed in a year. The data does not include tax filings made by proprietorships, partnerships, and limited liability companies. The RMA data is supplied primarily by commercial lenders and includes about 150,000 businesses. The Financial Studies of the Small Business is compiled from over 30,000 financial statements submitted by CPA firms.

How Representative is the Data?

Given the failure to include the population of non-corporate pass through entities in the sampling, a question may be raised about how representative the IRS data is of small closely held businesses.

Non IRS data sources may also not be representative because the data were not selected on a randomized or even stratified basis. Essentially the data includes those financial statements that CPA firms and commercial lenders choose to submit.

Aggregation Issues

In order to use ratio analysis as a benchmarking tool it is important to insure that comparisons are made between similar companies. This is a more difficult problem than you might imagine. First, there are different categorization systems used to classify the type of business a firm operates in. The most widely used traditional indexing system was the Standard Industrial Code (SIC). This has given way to a new system called the North American Industry Classification System (NAICS). The IRS has its own system which is a modified form of the SIC.

A second issue involves the size of operations. Most data bases breakdown companies based upon asset size. Such a classification scheme based upon assets reported on balance sheets using historical costs might not give a very good indication of a company's true size.

A third issue involves separating out companies with and without net income. Most data sources breakout their data in this way. The thought behind this is that aggregating profitable and not profitable businesses would lead to a distorted view of the profitable businesses. As you recall the distinction between a profitable and not profitable business may depend upon the classification of owner compensation as much as differences in economic performance. Certain firms considered as not profitable in a data base may in fact be profitable and vice-versa.

Answers to Selected Problems

2.1. Net income = $22,000. Total Assets = $57,400. Equity = $27,000.

3.1. Net income = $560. Total Assets = $5,560.

4.1. Net Income Cash Basis = $1,100. Net Loss Accrual Basis = $(100)

5.1. $200.

7.1. Annual computer depreciation expense = $500. Furniture depreciation expense = $2,000.

8.1. Ending inventory in units = 50. Ending Inventory Cost FIFO = $2,900, LIFO = $2,500, Weighted Average = $2,655. Costs of Goods Sold (CGS) FIFO = $10,375, LIFO = $10,775, Weighted Average = $10,620. Gross Profit FIFO = $9,625, LIFO = $9,225 and Weighted Average = $9,380.

9.1. Net Income = $69,540. Total Assets = $119,550. Total Liabilities = $40,010. Total Equity = $79,540.

10.1. Current Ratio = 2.68. Accounts Receivable Turnover = 17.7. Average Collection Period = 20.6 days. Inventory Turnover = 24.9.

Glossary

Accelerated Depreciation. A method of depreciation in which a greater amount of depreciation expense is recorded in the earlier years of an asset's useful life than in later years.

Accounts Receivable. A customer or client's promise to pay for goods or services provided.

Accounts. Sub-categories of assets, liabilities, equity, revenue and expense.

Accounts Payable. A firm's promise to pay a vendor for goods or services provided.

Accrual Basis of Accounting. The recognition of revenue when earned and expenses when incurred as distinguished from the cash basis of accounting.

Accumulated Depreciation. The contra asset account that reflects depreciation expense taken in the current and previous periods.

Aging Schedule. A schedule that classifies accounts receivable by the amount of days the receivable has been unpaid.

Assets. Tangible or intangible things that allow a firm to produce goods or services.

Audit. A set of tests and procedures applied by an independent accounting firm to determine the accuracy of financial statement information.

Balance Sheet. One of the basic financial statements that is used to asses the financial condition of a company. It lists the assets, liabilities and equity of the firm at the end of the accounting period.

Books of Original Entry. Specially designed forms on which transactions are initially recorded.

Business Firm. An organization established to earn a profit by selling of goods or services.

Cash Basis of Accounting. A system of accounting that recognizes revenue only when cash is received from customers or clients and expenses only when cash is paid to vendors.

Cash Flow Statement. A financial statement that reports cash flows from operating, financing and investing activities.

Corporations. A common form of limited liability firm

Cost of Goods Sold. The cost associated with selling goods (inventory).

Credits. Entries made on the right side of "T" accounts.

Debits. Entries made on the left side of "T" accounts.

Deferred Revenue. Cash collected from customers or clients prior to the delivery of goods and services.

Depreciation Expense. The portion of an asset's cost allocated to the current accounting period.

Dividends. Cash distributions from corporate profits to its shareholders.

Employee Bonding. Insurance against employee theft and embezzlement.

Equity. The difference between a firm's assets and its liabilities.

Expense. The use of resources to produce the goods and services sold to customers and clients.

FIFO. A flow assumption in valuing ending inventories that assumes that the first goods sold were the first ones purchased.

Fixed Asset Schedule. A record of a firm's assets that tracks acquisition dates and costs, depreciation methods used and cumulative amounts of depreciation taken.

Fixed Assets. Tangible assets such as machinery and equipment, furniture and fixtures and real property.

Generally Accepted Accounting Principles (GAAP). The most widely accepted rules of financial accounting.

Going Concern Value. The combined value of a firm's assets that would be paid by a purchaser who intended to continue operating the business.

Goodwill. The difference between a firm's going concern value and its liquidating value.

Gross Profit. The difference between sales and cost of goods sold.

Historical Cost Principle. The listing of asset values based upon their acquisition price rather than their current market value.

Income Statement. A basic financial statement that attempts to measure economic performance in the most recent accounting period. The statement reflects revenue and expenses.

Intangible Assets. Assets such as patents, trademarks and goodwill.

Internal Controls. The procedures used by a firm to protect its assets, insure reliability of its financial information and prevent fraud.

Inventory. Goods held by a firm for resale to its customers.

Lapping Schemes. Embezzlement schemes that involves the systematic misposting of customer and client payments.

Leverage. The degree to which a firm uses debt to finance its operations.

Liabilities. A firm's obligations to its creditors.

LIFO. (Last in, first out) An inventory flow assumption that assumes that the most recently sold inventory is also the most recently purchased.

Limited Liability Firms. Firms organized under special state statutes that insure that the owners' liabilities for the firm's actions are limited to their investment.

Liquidating Value. The amount that would be paid for a firm's assets on a piece meal basis.

Liquidity. The availability of cash in a business.

Loss. The excess of expenses over revenue.

Matching Concept. The idea behind accrual accounting that holds that revenue should be recognized at the same time as associated expenses are incurred.

Materiality. A threshold amount accountants utilize in deciding if adjustments are needed to a particular account.

Partnership. A form of unlimited liability firm with more than one owner.

Periodic Inventory Method. A method of recording inventory purchases that reflects adjustments to the inventory account only at the end of an accounting period.

Perpetual Inventory Method. A method of recording inventory purchases that changes the inventory account balance as purchases and sales are made.

Postings. The process of transferring transaction information recorded in books of original entry to general ledger "T" accounts.

Prepaid Expenses. A firm's payment to vendors for goods and services to be provided at some later point.

Price Index. A method of comparing the purchasing power of money over different time periods.

Profit. The excess of revenues over expenses.

Retained Earnings. Undistributed profits of a corporation.

Retainers. A form of deferred revenue collected by attorneys or other service businesses.

Revenue. Cash or receivables received from customers or clients in exchange for goods and services provided.

Segregation of Duties. An internal control which insures that employees with access to assets have no access to accounting records.

Shareholders. The owners of a corporation.

Sole Proprietorship. An unlimited liability firm with one owner.

Straight Line Depreciation. A method of depreciation expense that allocates an asset's purchase cost evenly over it's expected useful life.

Subsidiary Ledgers. Special records that detail the sales and payment histories for individual customers in the case of accounts receivable, or purchase and payment histories for individual vendors, in the case of accounts payable.

"T" Accounts. General ledger accounts that have a "T" format that clearly demarcate a left side and right side.

Transactions. Any events that cause a change in assets, liabilities, equity, revenue and expense.

Unlimited Liability Firms. Businesses whose owners remain liable for the actions of a business beyond the amount they actually invest.

Weighted Average Cost Method. An ending inventory valuation method based upon the weighted average of purchase costs during the accounting period.

Subject Index